CELEBRATING MICHAEL JACKSON

"Looking Back at the King of Pop"

1958-2009

By: Anelda Ballard

"One of His Biggest Fan's"

"When I saw him move I was mesmerized. I've never seen a performer perform like James Brown and right then and there I knew…that was what I wanted to do for the rest of my life." The Late Michael Jackson

Celebrating Michael Jackson
"Looking Back at the King of Pop"
1958-2009
By: Anelda Ballard
"One of His Biggest Fan's"

Cover design by: Aisha Meacham
Logo design by: Andre M. Saunders
Editor: September Summer
Co-Editor: Anelda Ballard
Photographs by: Internet, www.last.fm.com,

© 2009 Anelda Ballard

ISBN 978-0-9768540-9-8
ISBN 0-9768540-9-0

Information obtained from the internet, Allmusic Guide, www.philly.com, www.eLyrics.net, www.azlyrics.com, The Philadelphia Daily News www.imdb.com, www.en.wikipedia.com, www.guinnessworldrecord.com, www.allmichaeljackson.com, Maya Angelou's Poem "We Had Him", Facebook, Issecolor, www.last.fm.com, www.metrolyrics.com, www.msnbc.msn.com, and Steve Huey.

All rights reserved. This book is protected under the copyright laws of the United States of America. This book may not be copied or reprinted for commercial gain or profit. For Worldwide Distribution, printed in the United States of America. Published by Jazzy Kitty Greetings Marketing & Publishing, LLC. Utilizing Microsoft Publishing Software.

ACKNOWLEDGMENTS

I would like to acknowledge my entire staff at Jazzy Kitty Greetings Marketing & Publishing for helping me put this tribute together to honor the Late Michael Jackson. A special thank to Aisha for her ideas for the cover and daily contributions in researching Michael's life and music. She helped us to organize the project; and assisted in putting the entire manuscript together. She is almost as big of fan as I am.

Next I would like to thank my husband Ronald for his love and support for all of my long hours working and talking about it over and over again.

I want to thank my daughter MoNae, my mother Jean, my sister Marquita, my aunt Linda, my assistant Aisha, Katrina of Issecolor, and my First Lady Terri Pope of New Life Christian Center for your comments in the Fan Reactions section.

I want to also acknowledge the all fans on Facebook that reached out to me. And all of you around the world that love Michael. Because without you, I would not have known how much this book absolutely was needed.

DEDICATIONS

This book is dedicated to everyone who loves Michael Jackson. Simply put, it is dedicated to the fans and Michael's family.

Michael will never die; he will live forever in our hearts. His legacy will live on through his music. Michael, Rest in Peace (R.I.P.)

CELEBRATING MICHAEL JACKSON

"Looking Back at the King of Pop"

1958-2009

Introduction..	i
Poem "Gone Too Soon"..	01
Michael Jackson's Accomplishments/Autobiography...	03
His Trade Marks..	12
Important Facts about Michael Jackson..	12
Michael and His Brother's Go Animated...	13
The History of Michael Jackson's Music...	15
Thriller (In a Class by Itself)...	33
Michael Jackson on the Cover...	43
Fans Reactions...	44
Photo Album..	47
Some Popular Lyrics..	65
Poem "We Had Him" by Maya Angelou..	81
Reference/Footnotes..	83

INTRODUCTION

This book was written in hopes that it would keep Michael Jackson's memory alive. I wanted to give his fans the opportunity to take a moment to look back at Michael's life and reminisce about the positive times only. You will not read about any negative things in this book. You can turn on the TV, read the newspaper, a magazine or go on the internet for that.

We will go back to his childhood and go up until his untimely death on June 25, 2009. He passed way at the young age of 50 and it broke our hearts. I pray that something read or something seen will enlighten or touch your heart. We will look back at his music and more.

So let's start taking a look back and celebrate Michael Joseph Jackson's life that touched so many! The best entertainer, the true "King of Pop" and the most generous humanitarian that ever lived.

Michael Jackson Had 9 Siblings.

Michael was the eighth of the 10 children (3 sisters and 6 brothers) born to parents Joseph Walter Jackson and Katherine Esther. Michael Joseph Jackson (August 29, 1958 - June 25, 2009)

1. Maureen Reilette "Rebbie" Jackson (born May 29, 1950)
2. Sigmund Esco "Jackie" Jackson (born May 4, 1951)
3. Toriano Adaryll "Tito" Jackson (born October 15, 1953)
4. Jermaine LaJaune Jackson (born December 11, 1954)
5. La Toya Yvonne Jackson (born May 29, 1956)
6. Marlon David Jackson (born March 12, 1957)
7. Brandon Jackson (Twin born March 12, 1957 - died at birth)
8. Steven Randall "Randy" Jackson (born October 29, 1961)
9. Janet Damita Jo Jackson (born May 16, 1966)

(Michael also has a younger half sister Joh'Vonnie who is Joe's daughter with Cheryl Terrell.)

GONE TOO SOON

Your life was Cut Too Short

God, how we miss you

The news hit us like a brick

Everyone around the world cried…

Most of us couldn't stop the tears from falling from our eyes

And we fell on our knees

I know we are not suppose to question God

But we can't stop asking, WHY?

The news of your passing,

Practically left most of us cold

In fact, it almost killed us,

Because we know you're forever gone

We can't believe that on this earth

We won't see you again

It feels like we lost a best friend

We thank God for the memories,

Your legacy and your music

That you left us for 50 years

That is constantly in our heads

It will keep you alive daily and with us

Instead of forgotten and dead

(Continued)

GONE TO SOON

Know one knows how much each one of us is hurting

As we struggle with this loss

Know one knows how must pain it has cost

Every time I think of it, my heart drops!

The world lost the greatest entertainer and humanitarian that ever lived

We lost "the King of Pop"

Michael you're, Gone Too Soon

Your life was Cut Too Short

God, How we miss you

I don't know what we are going to do?

We will listen to your songs over and over again

I lost a piece of me on June 25th

I pray daily that this pain will soon end

My life will NEVER be the same

Maybe God needed you for something

That only you could do

Like to moonwalk in Heaven

Sing a special tune, even dance for Him;

Personally in the Upper Room

Because nothing else makes since

Your life was Cut Too Short

GONE TOO SOON

Michael Jackson's Accomplishments/Autobiography

Michael Joseph Jackson was born on August 29, 1958 in Gary, Indiana to Joseph Walter Jackson and Katherine Esther Jackson. He had 3 sisters and 6 brothers; Maureen Reilette "Rebbie" Jackson, Sigmund Esco "Jackie" Jackson, Toriano Adaryll "Tito" Jackson, Jermaine LaJaune Jackson, La Toya Yvonne Jackson, Marlon David Jackson, Brandon Jackson (Marlon's twin died at birth) Steven Randall "Randy" Jackson, Janet Damita Jo Jackson. Michael also has a younger half sister Joh'Vonnie who is Joe's daughter with Cheryl Terrell.

He debuted on the professional music scene at the age of 11 as a member of The Jackson 5. Michael displayed a talent for music and dance from an extremely young age. Michael Jackson was unquestionably the biggest and hottest pop star of the '80s, and certainly one of the most popular recording artists of all time. In his prime, Michael was an unstoppable and he possessed of all the tools to dominate the charts seemingly at will: an instantly identifiable voice, eye-popping dance moves, stunning musical versatility, and loads of sheer star power. His father Joe began to organize a family musical group around his three eldest sons in 1962. Michael joined them the following year, quickly establishing himself as a dynamic stage performer. His dead-on mastery of James Brown's dance moves and soulful, mature-beyond-his-years vocals made him a natural focal point, especially given his incredibly young age. The Jackson five became an opening act for such soul groups as the O-Jays and James Brown. It was Gladys Knight and Diana Ross who officially brought the group to Berry Gordy's attention. By 1969, and the boys were producing back-to-back chart-busting hits as Motown artists. The group signed to Motown in 1968 and issued their debut single in October 1969, when Michael was just 11 years old. "I Want You Back," "ABC," "The Love You Save," and "I'll Be There" all hit number one in 1970, making The Jackson 5 the first group in pop history to have their first four singles top the charts. In the early 1970s while still very young and a member of The Jackson 5, he appeared on "The Dating Game" in 1965. Roles were reversed; Michael asked the questions and picked a date from three eligible "bachelorettes".

Motown began priming Michael for a solo career in 1971, and his first single, "Got to Be There," was issued toward the end of the year; it hit the Top Five, as did the follow-up, a cover of Bobby Day's "Rockin' Robin."

Later in 1972, Michael had his first number one solo single, "Ben," the title song from a children's thriller about a young boy who befriends Ben, the highly intelligent leader of a gang of homicidal rats. Given the subject matter, the song was surprisingly sincere and sentimental, and even earned an Oscar nomination. He released his fourth and final album on Motown in 1975, and the following year, he and his brothers signed to Epic and became The Jacksons.

In 1977, Michael landed a starring role alongside Diana Ross in the all-African American film musical called The Wiz, a retelling of The Wizard of Oz. He met producer/composer Quincy Jones for the first time. Encouraged by the success of The Jacksons' self-produced, mostly self-written 1978 album Destiny, Michael elected to resume his solo career when his management contract with his father Joe expired shortly thereafter. With Jones producing him, Michael recorded his first solo album as an adult, Off the Wall. An immaculately crafted set of funky disco-pop, smooth soul, and sentimental pop ballads. Off the Wall made him a star all over again. It produced four Top Ten singles, including the number one hits "Don't Stop 'til You Get Enough" and "Rock With You," and went platinum (it went on to sell over seven million copies); even so, Michael remained loyal to his brothers and stayed with the group. He became an incredible American recording artist, entertainer, and businessman who are adored by many. When Michael performed in England in 1982, he asked to meet former actor Mark Lester. "He wanted to meet someone who had a similar background, a child star," Lester said. The result was a lifelong friendship and is godfather to his children. His 1982 blockbuster Thriller became the biggest-selling album of all time (probably his best-known accomplishment), and he was the first African American artist to find stardom on MTV, breaking down innumerable boundaries both for his race and for music video as an art form. No group could have contained Michael's rapidly rising star for long; however, there was still no sign (if there ever could be) that his next album would become the biggest in history. Released in 1982, the Quincy Jones-produced Thriller refined the strengths of Off the Wall; the dance and rock tracks were more driving, the pop tunes and ballads softer and more soulful, and all of it was recognizably Michael. He brought in Paul McCartney for a duet, guitarist Eddie Van Halen for a jaw-dropping solo, and Vincent Price for a creepy recitation. It was no surprise that Thriller was a hit; what was a surprise was its staying power. Thriller became the biggest-selling album of all time (probably his best-known accomplishment).

Michael's duet with McCartney, "The Girl Is Mine," was a natural single choice, and it peaked at number two; then "Billie Jean" and the Van Halen track "Beat It" both hit number one, for seven and three weeks respectively. Those latter two songs, as well as the future Top Five title track, had one important feature in common: Michael supported them with elaborately conceived video clips that revolutionized the way music videos were made. Michael treated them as song-length movies with structured narratives: "Billie Jean" set the song's tale of a paternity suit in a nightmarish dream world where Michael was a solitary, sometimes invisible presence; the anti-gang-violence "Beat It" became an homage to West Side Story; and the ten-minute-plus clip for "Thriller" (routinely selected as the best video of all time) featured Michael Jackson leading a dance troupe of rotting zombies, with loads of horror-film makeup and effects. Having never really accepted black artists in the past, MTV played the video frequently, garnering massive publicity for Michael Jackson and droves of viewers for the fledgling cable network.

Michael sealed his own phenomenon by debuting his signature "moonwalk" (who was taught by Jeffrey Daniels) dance step on May 16, 1983, on Motown's televised 25th anniversary special; though he didn't invent the moonwalk (as he himself was quick to point out), it became as much of a Michael signature as his vocal hiccups or single white-sequined glove. Showing no signs of slowing down, Thriller just kept spinning off singles, including "Wanna Be Startin 'Somethin'," the airy ballad "Human Nature," and "P.Y.T. (Pretty Young Thing)"; in all, seven of its nine tracks wound up in the Top Ten, obliterating conventional ideas of how many singles could be released from an album before it ran its course. Thriller stayed on the charts for over two years, spent 37 nonconsecutive weeks at number one, and became the best-selling album of all time; it went on to sell 25 million copies in the U.S. alone, and around another 20 million overseas. Naturally, Michael received many awards, including a record eight Grammys in one night, and got the largest endorsement deal ever when he became a spokesman for Pepsi (he would later be burned in an accident while filming a commercial).

At the end of 1983, Michael Jackson was again on top of the singles charts, this time as part of a second duet with McCartney, "Say Say Say."

In 1984, Michael rejoined his brothers one last time for the album Victory, whose supporting tour was one of the biggest (and priciest) of the year. 1984: Michael Jackson was burned in Pepsi ad. He received hospital treatment for serious burns to his head after his hair caught light during a freak filming accident. Michael shares with Carlos Santana and Norah Jones the record for most Grammys won in one year, with eight. He bought a large ranch, the name of his 2700-acre ranch near Santa Ynez, California, is Neverland Valley Ranch. It contains his house, an amusement park co-designed by Macaulay Culkin, a private theater and dance stage, and exotic animals. His estate contains a child's mini coaster, Zipper, Bumper cars, Merry go round, octopus, Giant slide and rocking dragon. There is also a full size basketball court; water wars section (for water gun fights) 2 Trains, (one steam train) and a zoo where he has various exotic animals including elephants, giraffes, alligators, a tiger and even an Anaconda(including the notorious pet chimpanzee Bubbles). President Ronald Reagan wanted to award a special White House medal to Michael Jackson, Bob Hope and the late John Wayne in 1984. However, future Chief Justice of the Supreme Court John Roberts advised against the proposal, saying the award was too much for a pop singer. He received a Presidential Humanitarian Award from President Reagan at the White House in May 1984, in recognition of Michael's contribution to the government's campaign against drunk driving.

In 1984, Michael Jackson revealed that he had a disorder called Vitiligo, in which pigment disappears from the skin, leaving large white blotches and making direct sunlight dangerous. Also, in 1984 he was the winner of the British Phonographic Industry Award for International Solo Artist to add to his accomplishments.

In 1985, he and Lionel Richie co-wrote the anthemia "We Are the World" for the all-star famine-relief effort USA for Africa; it became one of the fastest-selling singles ever. He acquired ATV Publishing, the firm that controlled all the Lennon-McCartney copyrights. Michael owned the rights to the Beatles' catalog; but he does not own the right to the entire Beatles catalogue. For example, the family of the late George Harrison own songs he wrote, including "Something," and Sony music owns 50% of the catalogue after Michael Jackson sold it to them. During his long layoff between records, Jackson indulged his interest in film and video by working with George Lucas and Francis Ford Coppola on the 3-D short film Captain EO. The special-effects extravaganza was shown at the enormous widescreen IMAX theaters in Disney's amusement parks for 12 years. Michael also won a poll of superstars to have his image on a stamp issued by the Virgin Islands in July 1985. He asked that the Virgin Islands donated all revenue (the stamps were priced between 60 cents and $1.50) to welfare and education.

In 1986, finally, Michael Jackson re-entered the studio with Quincy Jones to begin the near-impossible task of crafting a follow-up to Thriller. Bad was released to enormous public anticipation.

In 1987, it debuted at number one, and the first single, "I Just Can't Stop Loving You," with vocal accompaniment by Siedah Garrett, also shot up the charts to number one. Like Thriller, Bad continued to spin off singles for well over a year after its release, and became the first album ever to produce five number one hits; the others were "Bad," "The Way You Make Me Feel," "Man in the Mirror," and "Dirty Diana." Michael supported the album with a lengthy world tour that featured a typically spectacular, elaborate stage show; it became the highest-grossing tour of all time. Michael did not tour America after the BAD tour in 1987.

In July 1988, Michael was seen by a record 500,000 people during his seven day stand at Wembley Stadium. He has his look-alike puppet in the French show "Les guignols de l'info". Winner of the British Phonographic Industry Award for International Solo Artist in 1988. He was the highest earning singer of 1988-1989, with $125 million from his worldwide "BAD" album tour.

1989, Moonwalker was certified as the all-time top selling music video in March 1989. Michael was asked to write and perform the songs for Batman, but had to turn it down due to his concert commitments. He was presented with an "Artist of the Decade" award by Elizabeth Taylor in 1989, proclaiming him "the True King of Pop, Rock and Soul". He was also the Winner of the Brit Award for International Male in 1989.

Michael was honored by CBS as the "top selling act of the Eighties" in March 1990 and in April 1990; Michael attended the funeral of his close friend Ryan White who he wrote the song for Gone Too Soon. Ryan White was a hemophiliac teenager who died of AIDS-related illness in 1990 after contracting HIV through a blood transfusion. His mother has comments about Michael death in the fan reaction section. In return have written a poem "Gone Too Soon" Which is dedicated to Michael Jackson and his fans.

When Michael returned in with a new album in late 1991, he'd come up with a different moniker: "the King of Pop." Dangerous found Michael ending his collaboration with Quincy Jones in an effort to update his sound; accordingly, many of the tracks were helmed by the groundbreaking new jack swing producer Teddy Riley. As expected, the album debuted at number one, and its lead single, "Black or White," shot to the top as well.

In early 1992, Michael scored several more hits off the album, including the Top Tens "Remember the Time" and "In the Closet," but the aggressive "Jam" and the saccharine "Heal the World" both performed not as well as the others.

In the TV Drama The Jacksons: An American Dream in 1992 Michael Jackson is portrayed by Alex Burrall and Jason Weaver.

In January 1993, Michael performed during the halftime show at Super Bowl XXVII. It drew the largest viewing audience in the history of American television. He also performed at the ball for President Bill Clinton's first inauguration on January 20th. Michael Jackson married Lisa Marie Presley in 1994; they later divorced January 18, 1996.

In 1995, Michael attempted to put the focus back on his music by preparing HIStory: Past, Present and Future, Book 1, a two-CD set featuring one disc of new material and one of his greatest hits. The album debuted at number one, but the format did not go as well as Michael would have wanted: his fans already owned the hits, and the new album simply wasn't strong enough to offset the added cost of the extra disc for many more casual listeners. Although there were some encouraging signs -- the lead single "Scream," a duet with sister Janet, debuted at number five, setting a new American chart record that was broken when the follow-up, "You Are Not Alone," became the first single ever to enter the Billboard Hot 100 at number one. In 1996, He received a Special Award for a Generation at the Brit Awards in 1996. He received the World Music Award for world's best-selling album of all time, "Thriller", at the Monte Carlo Sporting Club, on May 8, 1996. Michael Jackson also got remarried, to nurse Debbie Rowe; and over the next two years, the couple had two children, son Prince Michael Jackson, Jr. and daughter Paris Michael Katherine Jackson. However, Michael Jackson and Debbie Rowe divorced October 8, 1999. Elizabeth Taylor is the Godmother of both his daughter Paris Jackson of his son Prince Michael Jackson I. Besides being godfather to Michael's first child Prince Michael Jackson I, Macaulay Culkin is also godfather to Jackson's daughter Paris Jackson. Michael was Godfather of Nicole Richie. In 1996, he also wrote and recorded a song called "On the Line", produced by Kenneth 'Babyface' Edmonds, for the film **Get on the Bus** that was not included on the soundtrack for the film.

In 1997 a survey declared Michael Jackson the most famous person in the world, ahead of Pope John Paul II and then US President Bill Clinton.

In January 2000 Michael announced he was considering retiring from the music industry, citing his weariness at publicity as a reason.

March 6, 2001, Michael addressed the Oxford Union on the subject of child welfare and his new initiative "Heal the Kids". In 2001, Michael Jackson was inducted into the Rock and Roll Hall of Fame, and later held a massive concert at Madison Square Garden celebrating the 30th anniversary of his first solo record Among many other celebrity guests, the show featured the first on-stage reunion of the Jacksons since the Victory tour. In the wake of September 11, Michael put together an all-star charity benefit single, "What More Can I Give." His new album, Invincible, was released late in the year, marking the first time he'd issued a collection of entirely new material since Dangerous; it found him working heavily with urban soul production wizard Rodney Jerkins. Invincible debuted at number one and quickly went double platinum, feature the singles, "You Rock My World" and "Butterflies". 2003 with one new song, "One More Chance". A Year later - nearly to the day - the four CD and one DVD box set The Ultimate Collection appeared with numerous rarities including the original demo for "We Are the World". Also, the TV documentary, "Living with Michael Jackson," aired. He discussed his loving relationship with children. He also told the interviewer that he love to climb trees, have water balloon fights and loves Peter Pan which inspires him. He took also took him to his favorite store to shop. Although Michael was not completely pleased with the interview.

Michael Jackson holds numerous Guinness World Records including the most Grammy Awards won in a year, most hit singles in the UK charts in a year, best selling album of all time, longest span of No.1 hits by an R&B artist, best selling music video, highest annual earnings ever for a pop star, and most successful pop music family. Held his first live concert in four years at Madison Square Garden, New York, in early September 2001.

In 2002 Michael Jackson, had planned to produce and star in the movie "The Nightmares of Edgar Allan Poe", about the last years of writer Edgar Allan Poe. He was to star as the famed 19th century author (who was Caucasian), and had written music for the film as well. He was inducted into the Songwriters Hall of Fame. April 24, 2002, "Beat It" was used in television advertisements. Michael joined Chris Tucker, Tony Bennett, former president Bill Clinton and members of the Democratic National Committee at Harlem's Apollo Theatre in New York for a concert fundraiser. Tucker co-hosted the event with actress Cicely Tyson, while Rubén Blades, K.D. Lang and Bennett performed. Michael sang a medley of songs that included "Black or White" and "Smooth Criminal," and was joined by Jane's Addiction guitarist and former Red Hot Chili Pepper Dave Navarro for a portion of his set.

On 13 June 2003, the day after his neighbor and friend of 25 years Gregory Peck died, Michael went to Peck's house to help his widow plan the memorial service. Peck had once publicly praised the singer as a model parent. In September 2003, for a charity event held at the Neverland Ranch, for the first time ever, he invited an artist from the outside to perform there. It was Yannick Harrison, also known as Jay Kid, from Denmark that performed a number of his interpretations of Michael Jackson songs for the specially invited guests.

In August 2004, He attended a memorial service for the late actor Marlon Brando in, along with Warren Beatty, Jack Nicholson and Sean Penn. Inducted into the UK Music Hall of Fame for his outstanding contribution to British music and integral part of British music culture on November 11th.

In January 2005, Michael soon relocated to the Persian Gulf island of Bahrain and began working on new music including a charity single that would benefit victims of Hurricane Katrina entitled, "I Have This Dream". Ciara, Snoop Dogg, R. Kelly, Keyshia Cole, James Ingram, Michael Jackson's brother Jermaine Jackson, Shanice, the Shirley Caesar and The O'Jays all supposedly lent their voices to the charity song. At the time, Michael's spokesperson, Raymone K. Bain, said the list of performers included Mary J. Blige, 'Missy 'Misdemeanor' Elliott', Jay-Z, James Brown and Lenny Kravitz. All of these artists later appeared to be no longer participating. More than a year later, the Katrina Charity Single remains unreleased. In 2006 the box set was released featuring 20 Dual Discs replicating 20 big hit singles with their videos included on the DVD side. May 27, 2006, Michael accepted a Legend Award at MTV Japan's VMA Awards in Tokyo. The award was honoring his influence and impact in music videos over the past 25 years. He received the Diamond Award for selling more than 100 million albums at the World Music Awards in London on November 15th and on December 30th He attended James Brown's funeral in Augusta, Georgia.

On March 10 2007, Michael greeted thousands of US troops in a US army base south of Tokyo it was about 3,000 troops and their family members gathered in a fitness center at Camp Zama. After Michael shaking hands with and thanking the troops personally for their service, he spoke to the crowd gathered, saying, and "Those of you in here today are some of the most special people in the world. It is because of you in here today, and others who so valiantly have given their lives to protect us, that we enjoy our freedom." He also attended a ceremony at the camp for an army member being promoted and put a pin on his uniform. Also early in 2007 it was announced that a comeback album was planned for late in the year.

In 2008 Michael painfully sells Neverland Ranch and he announces that he will be performing a series of 50 concerts in London. Tickets were sold out within 4 hours. Later In a press conference Michael told fans, "I love you so much." "Um…Thank you all. This is it. This is it." "I just want to say, that these…these will be my final show performance in London." "This is it, this is it….And when I say, this is it; I really mean, this is it." "Because um (He chuckles, looks down and away from the crowd, grabs his heart with admiration then continues) I'll be performing all of the songs my fans want to hear…this is it, I mean, this is it, I mean, this is really it, this is the final curtain call, okay?" "And um, I'll see you in July…And (long pause because the crowd is screaming) I love you so much, really…from the bottom of my heart. This is it…See you in July." Then Michael rises up his hands. The first show was scheduled on July

8th. On June 25, 2009, Los Angeles Fire Department (LAFD) paramedics received a 911 call at 12:21 pm (19:21 UTC), and arrived three minutes and seventeen seconds later, at which point Michael was reportedly not breathing. The recording of the emergency call was released by the LAFD on June 27, 2009. Paramedics are reported to have wanted to pronounce him dead at the scene, but a doctor insisted he be taken to a hospital. CPR was performed on the way to the Ronald Reagan UCLA Medical Center, where they arrived at 1:14 pm (20:14 UTC), and continued for an hour. He was pronounced dead at 2:26 pm (21:26 UTC). Michael Joseph Jackson dies of cardiac arrest. The news of his death spread quickly online, causing websites to crash and slows down from user overload. Both TMZ and the Los Angeles Times, two websites that were the first to confirm the news, suffered outages. He leaves behind his three children, Paris Michael Katherine Patricia Jackson born on April 3, 1998, Prince Michael Joseph Jackson Jr. born on February 13, 1997 and Prince Michael II Born in 2002 (aka Blanket B). His parents Joseph and Katherine, His sisters and brothers Rebbie Jackson, Jackie Jackson, Tito Jackson, Jermaine Jackson, La Toya Jackson, Marlon Jackson, Randy Jackson and Janet Jackson. He was the Uncle of Jermaine Jackson II, Valencia Jackson, Brittany Jackson, Marlon Jackson Jr., and Stevanna Jackson. Michael Jackson's superstar's funeral service was held at the AFG Staples Center in Los Angeles on Tuesday morning July 7, 2009. Tickets for some lucky fans were held in a lottery, others had to stay home and watch. The Home Going Services was heartfelt. Michael family had a private ceremony at Forrest Lawn where he will also be buried (that was not announced until August 18th and he was laid to rest on his birthday August 29th). The Staples Center Michael Jackson memorial service non-performing VIP attendees included Sean 'P. Diddy' Combs, Larry King, Barbara Walters, Jaleel White, 'Kimberly 'Lil' Kim' Jones' , Spike Lee, Don King, Vicki Roberts, Nicole Richie, Dionne Warwick, Kimberly Kardashian, and Kris Jenner to name a few. His gold coffin seen at his memorial is a rare design called the Promethean. It cost $25,000 and is made of solid bronze but is 14-carat gold-plated with a hand-polished mirror finish and lined with velvet. It is identical to the coffin used to bury James Brown in 2006 - which may have inspired Jackson after he saw it when Brown lay in state. MTV and BET began airing his music videos, and ran two news specials, until 8 p.m. EDT the following day of his death. An Amazon spokesperson said that the website sold out of all of his CDs, and those of the Jackson 5, within minutes of the news of his death breaking. His death triggered an outpouring of grief around the world, creating surges of Internet traffic and resulting in soaring album sales.

HIS TRADE MARKS - The Moonwalk. Single sequined white glove. He wore white socks with black shoes.

IMPORTANT FACTS ABOUT MICHAEL JACKSON

- His favorite movie as a child and teenager was Oliver (1968).
- Childhood school friend was David Gest.
- The Elephant Man (1980) was one of his favorite movies.
- An Andy Warhol head-and-shoulders portrait of him made the cover of Time magazine on 3/19/84.
- Michael's favorite "Beatles' song is "Come Together".
- Tatum O'Neal was Jackson's first girlfriend and allegedly his first real love.
- Michael and Brooke Shields are great friends.
- He was the ex-brother-in-law of James DeBarge.
- He is the godfather of Michael Gibb, son of The Bee Gees front man Barry Gibb. He was present at the private funeral service for Maurice Gibb.
- Michael Jackson was a frequent guest at the infamous "Studio 54"
- Recorded an anti-war song about the US invasion of Iraq, "We've Had Enough", which was included on his greatest hits package "Michael Jackson: The Ultimate Collection".
- He returned to live in the United States on 12/24/06, setting up residence in Las Vegas.
- At his peak, he was reportedly worth around $700 million and was recognized in the Guinness Book of World Records as the king of charity, giving an estimated $500 million.
- Is a fan of the Ultimate Fighting Championship.
- The Jacksons were awarded a Star on the Hollywood Walk of Fame for Recording at 1500 Vine Street in Hollywood, California and has sold over 300 million records worldwide.
- Producer Keya Morgan gave Jackson a ring that once belonged to Marilyn Monroe.
- He had been scheduled to perform 50 sold-out concerts to over one million people at London's O2 arena, from July 13, 2009 to March 6, 2010, which he implied during a press conference would have been the final concerts of his career. Following the week of his death, his album sales collectively spiked over 2000%. Music website Amazon sold as many Jackson albums in the 24 hours after his death as in the previous 11 years. His memorial service from the Staples Center on Tuesday, July 7th 2009 brought the Internet's second largest day ever in terms of total traffic.

MICHAEL AND HIS BROTHER'S GO ANIMATED

Format	The Jackson 5 Animated TV Series
Voices of	Paul Frees (Berry Gordy/Additional voices) Donald Fullilove (Michael) Edmund Sylvers (Marlon) Joel Cooper (Jermaine) Mike Martinez (Tito) Craig Grandy (Jackie) Diana Ross (Diana)
Country of Origin	United States

Production/Broadcast	
Producer(s)	Arthur Rankin, Jr. and Jules Bass
Running Time	30 min. No. of - Episodes 23
Production Co.(s)	Rankin/Bass Productions and Motown Productions
Original Channel/Run	ABC/September 11, 1971 – September 1, 1973

The Jackson 5ive was a Saturday morning cartoon series produced by Rankin/Bass and Motown Productions on ABC from September 11, 1971 until September 1, 1973; a fictionalized portrayal of the careers of Motown recording group The Jackson 5. ABC rebroadcast the series during the 1984 -1985 Saturday morning season, which were also the years when Michael Jackson had been riding a wave of popularity. The series was animated mainly in London at the studios of Halas and Batchelor. Some animation was done at Estudios Moro, Barcelona, Spain. The director was Spanish-American Robert Balser. Other than appearing in the introduction where actual photographs are shown morphing into animated cartoons, the actual Jackson brothers themselves - Jackie, Tito, Jermaine, Marlon, and

Michael - were unable to contribute to the show in any way due to scheduling conflicts. Only their music was used; however, during the music montages, a clipping of the Jackson 5 appearing in concert would air occasionally to blend in with the cartoon. Though Berry Gordy/The J5's producer did not provide the original voice (his character was voiced by Paul Frees), his character was frequently involved as the "adult figure" to the group. R&B/Pop singer Diana Ross contributed to voice her fictionalized self in the debut episode. The premise of the show is that the Jackson Five would have adventures similar to Josie and the Pussycats, Alvin & The Chipmunks or The Partridge Family, with the unique addition being that Berry Gordy, the manager of the band in the show's universe, would come up with an idea for publicity for the band, such as having to do farm work or play a concert for the President of the United States. A specially recorded medley of four Jackson 5 #1 hits - "I Want You Back", "The Love You Save", "ABC", and "Mama's Pearl"- served as the show's theme song. Each episode would feature 2 songs by the Jackson 5. The songs were derived from their albums Diana Ross Presents The Jackson 5, ABC, Maybe Tomorrow, and Third Album (with the exception of their cover of the song "Bridge Over Troubled Water"). In the newer episodes from 1972-73, songs were derived from Michael Jackson's album Got to Be There and two songs from the Lookin' Through the Windows album. Because Michael Jackson owned many pets in real life, a few pets were added as extra characters to the cartoon. They included Michael's pet mice, Ray and Charles (alluding to singer Ray Charles), and his pet snake Rosey. Other than the mice chirping, the pets never spoke, but usually either attributed to assistance, mischief or joining the Jackson Brothers in performances on the show.

Episodes Season 1

1. "It All Started With..."
2. "Pinestock U.S.A."
3. "Drafted"
4. "Mistaken Identity"
5. "Bongo, Baby Bongo"
6. "The Winner's Circle"
7. "Cinderjackson"
8. "The Tiny Five"
9. "The Groovatron"
10. "Ray and Charles: Superstars"
11. "The Wizard of Soul"
12. "Jackson Island"
13. "Farmer Jacksons"
14. "The Michael Look"
15. "Jackson Street, U.S.A."
16. "Rasho-Jackson"
17. "A Rare Pearl"

Season 2 (billed as The New Jackson 5ive Show)

1. "Who's Hoozis?"
2. "Michael White"
3. "Groove To The Chief"
4. "Michael In Wonderland"
5. "Jackson and The Beanstalk"
6. "The Opening Act"

THE HISTORY OF MICHAEL JACKSON'S MUSIC

MICHAEL JACKSON became a music industry legend in his own time. His collections of albums are award winning, and he has broken all the records. This is a discography of the records he released as a child star with his brothers The Jackson 5 and later as a young solo artist and then as an adult super star! From the 1969 Motown release of Diana Ross Presents The Jackson 5 to the 2009 pre-release of the live album set of One Night in Japan. DIANA ROSS PRESENTS THE JACKSON 5 - Motown - 12/1969 - 12 Tracks - Groups debut album - Includes: I WANT YOU BACK. -DIANA ROSS PRESENTS THE JACKSON 5- ABC - Motown - 2/1970 - 12 Tracks - Eventually sold 6 million world wide! Includes: ABC, THE LOVE YOU SAVE. -ABC- THIRD ALBUM - Motown - 9/1970 - 11 Tracks - Groups highest selling album at 6 million

worldwide. Includes: I'LL BE THERE, MAMA'S PEARL.-THIRD ALBUM- THE JACKSON 5 CHRISTMAS ALBUM – Motown - 10/15/1970 - 12 tracks only holiday release by Motown. Sales topped 3 million worldwide. Includes: - SANTA CLAUS IS COMING TO TOWN, GIVE LOVE ON CHRISTMAS DAY. -**THE JACKSON 5 CHRISTMAS ALBUM**-MAYBE TOMORROW - Motown - 4/1971 - 11 Tracks - Sales of this mostly ballads album topped 4 million worldwide. Includes: NEVER CAN SAY GOODBYE, MAYBE TOMORROW.- MAYBE TOMORROW-GOIN BACK TO INDIANA - Motown - 9/1971 - 9 Tracks - Live soundtrack recording of an ABC-TV special along with live recordings from a 5/29/1971 Gary Indiana "homecoming" concert. Sold 2.5 million copies worldwide. Includes: GOIN BACK TO INDIANA.-GOIN BACK TO INDIANA- **GOT TO BE THERE** - Motown - 1/1972 - 10 Tracks – This was the first solo album for Michael Jackson with his brothers. Michael was 13 at the time. Includes: ROCKIN ROBIN, GOT TO BE THERE, WANNA BE WHERE YOU ARE.-GOT TO BE THERE- LOOKIN' THROUGH THE WINDOWS - Motown - 1972 - 11 Tracks - This album release marked the beginning of some of the well know discord between the group and Motown. Includes: LITTLE BITTY PRETTY ONE, LOOKIN, THROUGH THE WINDOWS, to name a few. BEN –

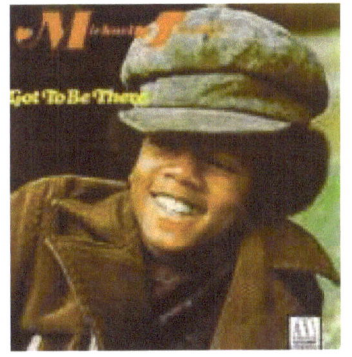

Motown - 8/4/1972 - 10 Tracks - This album marked Michael's second solo album and his first million seller hit in the U.S. with the title song **BEN**. Includes BEN. - YOU CAN CRY ON MY SHOULDER- Motown - 3/1973 - 10 Tracks - By this time the brothers tried to change their music and were prevented by Motown. This is one of the least successful albums the Jackson brothers ever created mainly because of only one top twenty single, and lack of promotion because they were on a worldwide tour at this time. This would be the last album that followed the bubblegum pop sound, and from this point on, the group would follow a more soulful disco sound. Includes: CORNER OF THE SKY, HALLELUJAH DAY- SKYWRITER-MUSIC AND ME - Motown - 4/13/1973 - 10 Tracks - As frustration grew over Motown's restrictions on the groups creativity this album also suffered from less direct promotion. Also the music landscape of society was changing as Michael's voice was also growing into that of a man. Includes: WITH A CHILDS HEART.-MUSIC AND ME- GET IT TOGETHER - Motown - 9/1973 - 8 Tracks - By this time

disagreement with Motown was growing. Material was becoming harder to develop. The group was further transitioning from "bubble gum pop" to more of a "funk and disco" sound. All the groups' voices were changing. **DANCING MACHINE** became a #2 pop hit. Includes: GET IT TOGETHER, DANCING MACHINE.-GET IT TOGETHER- IN JAPAN - Motown - 10/1973 - 12 Tracks - Culled from a live concert held in Japan in 1973. Motown did not release the album in the United States until 2004. By 1973, The Jackson 5 were bigger worldwide than they were in America. Features many of their earlier hit records, as well as solo hits from

members Michael Jackson and Jermaine Jackson. Includes: MEDLEY-"I WANT YOU BACK"/"ABC"/"THE LOVE YOU SAVE" -IN JAPAN- DANCING MACHINE - Motown - 9/1974 - 9 Tracks - The brothers still complained of their artistic direction. Nonetheless, the album became another disco concept album for the group, and show-cased lead singers Michael and Jermaine Jackson. Includes the songs: WHATEVER YOU GOT I WANT, I AM LOVE and DANCING MACHINE. **FOREVER MICHAEL** – "One Day in Your Life" is a song recorded by Michael Jackson for his 1975 album, Forever, Michael. It was later released as

a single in 1981 due to the strong buzz that generated from the sales of Jackson's hit 1979 album Off the Wall, even though Jackson released that album on a different label. While a modest U.S. hit, it was a bigger hit in the UK, where it became Jackson's first solo recording to hit #1 on the UK Singles Chart. It was number one in the UK for 2 weeks in June 1981, succeeding "Being with You" by Smokey Robinson. This song also featured strongly on the South African singles charts. It was released on the Motown label. It went on to become the 6th best-selling single of 1981 in the UK. Motown - 1/16/1975 - 10 Tracks. This album was Michael's fourth as a solo artist. Also Michael's last solo album released with Motown. It Includes: ONE DAY IN YOUR LIFE, JUST A LITTLE BIT OF YOU, WE'RE ALMOST THERE.-FOREVER MICHAEL - MOVING VIOLATION - Motown - 5/1975 - **10 Tracks** - This album would be the ninth and last studio album with Motown after six years with the label. It sold 1.6 million worldwide. Michael was now 16. This would be an early disco/funk release. Leaving Jermaine Jackson at Motown the group went on to sign with CBS records after adding youngest brother Randy. To avoid legal problems with Motown they renamed themselves **"The Jacksons"**. Includes:

FOREVER CAME TODAY, ALL I DO IS THINK OF YOU, BODY LANGUAGE.-MOVING VIOLATION- THE BEST OF MICHAEL JACKSON-Motown-1975-10 Tracks-This is a compilation of Michael Jacksons hits while at Motown. It sold 2.2 million worldwide. **THE BEST OF MICHAEL JACKSON-THE JACKSONS**-CBS-11/1976- 10 tracks- For the first time the group was allowed to write their own songs, unlike at Motown. This was the groups' first "gold" album despite selling 10 million records while at Motown. The first song written and published by Michael "BLUES AWAY" was published on this album. Includes: SHOW YOU THE WAY TO GO. Destiny is a 1978 album released by American band The Jacksons on the CBS/Epic Records label. The band had left their longtime label Motown in 1975 with the exception of brother Jermaine Jackson who had stayed with Motown after he married Berry Gordy's daughter, Hazel Gordy. After a couple of years signed with Philly International, The Jacksons now set their sights on one of CBS Records' most popular labels, Epic. After their last two CBS albums were spearheaded by legendary producers Kenny Gamble and Leon Huff, Epic allowed the Jackson brothers to write and produce their own material fully for the first time in their career. Composing much of the album in their home-made recording studio in their gated Hayvenhurst mansion, the group finished recording the album within two months. Like many of the acts that had left Motown, The Jacksons had to accept the possibility that they would no longer enjoy the same level of success they had while they were associated with the label-something Motown itself reiterated upon hearing that longtime front man Michael Jackson had moved onto a full-fledged solo career following Destiny's release. The album's lead single, "Blame It On The Boogie", was written by Mick Jackson, an English writer/performer who had his own version of the song in the UK charts at the same time as The Jacksons. It was The Jacksons' version, however, that was the more successful and is consequently the best known rendition of the song. Released on December 17, 1978, Destiny re-established them as a top-selling group. The album's success was largely based on the second single released from the album, "Shake Your Body (Down to the Ground)", which became a Top 10 single in the spring of 1979. The single, "Blame It on the Boogie", was also released. The album eventually peaked at number eleven on the Billboard Pop Albums chart and number three on the Billboard Black Albums chart and went on to platinum status cementing it as the first RIAA-certified platinum seller by The Jacksons as most of their Motown recordings were uncertified, despite their huge success on the charts. The accompanying tour was a huge success running on many legs and also

toured overseas. In honor of its 30th anniversary, **DESTINY**, including two bonus tracks of rare 12-inch disco mixes previously unavailable on CD was released on January 27, 2009 on Epic/Legacy, an Entertainment.[1]

TRACK LISTING All songs written by The Jacksons except where notified "Blame It on the Boogie" (Mick Jackson/David Jackson/E. Krohn)-3:36 "Push Me Away"-4:19 "Things I Do For You"-4:05 "Shake Your Body (Down to the Ground)" (Michael Jackson/Randy Jackson) 8:00 "Destiny" 4:55 "Bless His Soul"[1]-4:57 "All Night Dancin'" (Michael Jackson/Randy Jackson)-6:11 "That's What You Get (For Being Polite)" (Michael Jackson/Randy Jackson)-4:57 "Blame It on the Boogie" (John Luongo Disco Mix)*-6:59 "Shake Your Body (Down to the Ground)" (John Luongo Disco Mix)*-8:38 **THE WIZ** is a 1978 musical film produced by

---

[1] LegacyRecordings.com » News

Motown Productions and Universal Pictures, and released by Universal on October 24, 1978. An urbanized retelling of L. Frank Baum's The Wonderful Wizard of Oz featuring an entirely African-American cast, The Wiz was adapted from the 1975 Broadway musical of the same name. The film follows the adventures of Dorothy, a shy schoolteacher from Harlem, New York who finds herself magically transported to the wonderland of Oz, which resembles a fantasy version of New York City. Befriended by a Scarecrow, a Tin Man, and a Cowardly Lion, Dorothy travels through the world of Oz to seek an audience with the mysterious "Wiz", who they say has the power to take her home. Produced by Rob Cohen and directed by Sidney Lumet, The Wiz stars Diana Ross, Michael Jackson, Nipsey Russell, Ted Ross, Mabel King, Theresa Merritt, Thelma Carpenter, Lena Horne, and Richard Pryor. The film's story was reworked from William F. Brown's Broadway libretto by Joel Schumacher, and Quincy Jones supervised the adaptation of Charlie Smalls and Luther Vandross' songs for film. A handful of new songs, written by Jones and the songwriting team of Nickolas Ashford & Valerie Simpson, were added for the film version. Upon its original theatrical release, the Wiz received four Academy Award nominations for Best Art Direction, Best Costume Design, Best Original Music Score and Best Cinematography.

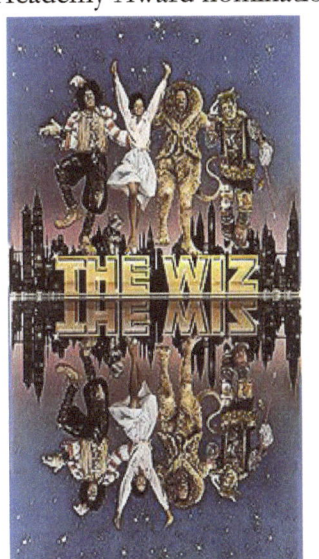

CAST, Actor Diana Ross, Role Dorothy Gale, Actor Michael Jackson, Role Scarecrow, Actor Lena Horne, Role Glinda, The Good Witch of the South, Actor Ted Ross, Role Cowardly Lion, Actor Nipsey Russell, Role Tin Man, Actor Thelma Carpenter, Role Miss One, the Good Witch of the North, Actor Theresa Merritt, Role Aunt Em, Actor Stanley Greene Role Uncle Henry **Actor** Richard Pryor Role The Wiz, **Actor** Mabel King Evillene, Role, The Wicked Witch of the West SONGS All songs written by Charlie Smalls, unless otherwise noted. 1."Overture Part I" (instrumental),"Overture Part II" (instrumental) 2. "The Feeling That We Had"-Aunt Emma and Chorus 3. "Can I Go On?" (Quincy Jones, Nickolas Ashford and Valerie Simpson) - Dorothy "Tornado"/"Glinda's Theme" (instrumental) 4. "He's The Wizard"-Miss One and Chorus "Soon As I Get Home"/"Home"-Dorothy 5. "You Can't Win, You Can't Break Even"-Scarecrow and The Four Crows 6. "Ease On Down The Road #1"-Dorothy and Scarecrow 7. "What Would I Do If I Could Feel?"-Tin Man 8. "Slide Some Oil to Me"-Tin Man 9. "Ease On Down The Road #2"-Dorothy, Scarecrow, and Tin Man 10. "I'm A Mean Ole Lion"-Cowardly Lion 11. "Ease On Down The Road #3"-Dorothy, Scarecrow, Tin

Man, and Cowardly Lion 12. "Poppy Girls Theme" (Anthony Jackson) (instrumental) 13. "Be a Lion"-Dorothy, Scarecrow, Tin Man, and Cowardly Lion "End of the Yellow Brick Road" (instrumental) 14. "Emerald City Sequence" (music: Jones, lyrics: Smalls) - Chorus 15. "Is This What Feeling Gets? (Dorothy's Theme)" (music: Jones, lyrics: Ashford & Simpson) - Dorothy (vocal version not used in film) 16. "Don't Nobody Bring Me No Bad News"- Abilene and the Winkies 17. "Everybody Rejoice/A Brand New Day" (Luther Vandross) - Dorothy, Scarecrow, Tin Man, Cowardly Lion, and Chorus 18. "If You Believe In Yourself (Dorothy)"- Dorothy "The Good Witch Glinda" (instrumental) 19. "If You Believe In Yourself (Reprise)" - Glinda the Good Witch 20. "Home (Finale)"- Dorothy **OFF THE WALL** is the fifth studio album by the American pop musician Michael Jackson, released August 10, 1979 on Epic Records, after his well received film performance in The Wiz. While working on that project, Jackson and Quincy Jones had become friends, and Jones agreed to work with Jackson on his next studio album. Recording sessions took place between December 1978 and June 1979 at Allen Zentz

Recording, Westlake Recording Studios, and Cherokee Studios in Los Angeles, California. Michael collaborated with a number of other writers and performers such as Paul McCartney, Stevie Wonder and Rod Temperton. He wrote several of the songs himself, including the lead single, "Don't Stop 'til You Get Enough". The record was a departure from Jackson's previous work for Motown. Several critics observed that Off the Wall was crafted from funk, disco-pop, soul, soft rock, jazz and pop ballads. Jackson received positive reviews for his vocal performance on the record. The record gained positive reviews and won the singer his first Grammy Awards since the early 1970s. With Off the Wall, Jackson became the first solo artist to have four singles from the same album peak inside the top 10 of the Billboard Hot 100. The album was a commercial success, to date it is certified for 7× Multi-Platinum in the US and has sold 20 million copies worldwide. On October 16, 2001, a special edition reissue of Off the Wall was released by Sony Records. Recent reviews by Allmusic and Blender have continued to praise Off the Wall for its appeal in the 21st century. In 2003, the album was ranked number 68 on Rolling Stone magazine's list

of the 500 greatest albums of all time. The National Association of Recording Merchandisers listed it at number 80 of the Definitive 200 Albums of All Time. In 2008, Off the Wall was inducted into the Grammy Hall of Fame. **TRACK LISTING** "Don't Stop 'til You Get Enough"

Writer(s) Michael Jackson Length 6:05, "Rock with You" Writer(s) Rod Temperton Length 3:40 "Workin' Day and Night" Writer(s) Jackson Length 5:14 "Get on the Floor" Writer(s) Jackson, Louis Johnson Length 4:06 "Girlfriend" Writer(s) Paul McCartney Length 3:05 "She's out of My Life" Writer(s) Tom Bahler Length 3:05 "I Can't Help It" Writer(s) Susaye Greene, Stevie Wonder Length 4:28 "It's the Falling in Love" (with Patti Austin) Writer(s) David Foster, Carole Bayer Sager Length 3:48 "Burn This Disco Out" Writer(s) Temperton Length 3:40 **THRILLER** - Epic - 11/30/1982 - 9 Tracks - Sixth studio album released by Michael Jackson. **(SEE THRILLER IS IN A CLASS BY ITSELF)**. Drafted into a distinctive rock guitar solo. Following the successful chart performances of Thriller, "The Girl Is Mine" and "Billie Jean", "Beat It" was released on February 14, 1983, as the album's third

single. The song was a worldwide commercial and critical success, becoming one of the best-selling singles of all time. Both "Billie Jean" and "Beat It" occupied Top 5 positions at the same time, a feat matched by very few artists. Cited as one of the most lauded songs in history, "Beat It" was certified platinum in 1989. Honored numerous times- including two Grammy Awards, two American Music Awards and an induction into the Music Video Producers Hall of Fame - "Beat It" and the song's corresponding music video propelled Thriller into becoming the best-selling album of all time. The song was promoted with a short film that featured Jackson bringing two gangs together through the power of dance. Covered and sampled by modern artists, including Fergie and Fall Out Boy, "Beat It" was included in the National Highway Safety Commission's anti-drink driving campaign. Prior to Jackson's death, "Beat It" became a signature piece for the singer; he performed it on all of his world tours. On July 4, 1984, Jackson performed "Beat It" live with his brothers during The Jacksons' Victory Tour. The brothers were joined on stage by Eddie Van Halen, who played the guitar in his solo spot. The song became a signature song of Jackson; the singer performed it on all of his world tours; Bad,

Dangerous and HIStory. The October 1, 1992 Dangerous Tour performance of "Beat It" was included on the DVD of the singer's Michael Jackson: The Ultimate Collection box set. The DVD was later repackaged as Live in Bucharest: The Dangerous Tour. Jackson also performed the song on the Michael Jackson: 30th Anniversary Special, a concert celebrating the musician's thirtieth year as a solo performer. The performance featured Slash as the song's guest guitarist.

FAREWELL MY SUMMER LOVE - Motown - 5/18/1984 9 Tracks - A compilation of unreleased archived Michael Jackson recordings from 1973 until 1975. Includes: YOU'VE REALLY GOT A HOLD ON ME. - **FAREWELL MY SUMMER LOVE**. **Farewell My Summer Love** (originally titled **Farewell My Summer Love 1984** and later re-issued as Here I Am (Come and Take Me) in the UK) was a compilation of unreleased archived Michael Jackson recordings from 1973 until 1975. The album was released by Motown Records in the U.S. on May 15, 1984 as a "lost" Michael Jackson solo album that was meant to be released in 1974 but was later held off because of The Jackson 5's renewed success with "Dancing Machine. "The nine songs featured on the album were originally recorded in 1973 but had not been previously released. To give the album a more 1980s sound, Motown remixed the songs and added all new musical overdubs. The task of playing the updated sound was given to musicians Tony Peluso, Michael Lovesmith and Steve Barri. Together with drummer Mike Baird, they recorded new guitar, keyboard, and percussion drum parts for the songs. The album reached #46 on Billboard's pop album chart and #9 on the UK albums chart. The title track was also released as a single in May, 1984. It became a Top 40 hit in the US, reaching #38, and a Top 10 hit in the United Kingdom, reaching #7. At the time, Jackson was riding high on the success of his best-selling Thriller album. A follow up single, "Girl You're So Together" was a top 40 hit in the UK. Like One Day in Your Life, Farewell My Summer Love has never seen a re-release, although the title track is available on several of Jackson's greatest hits collections. In particular, Motown's comprehensive Michael Jackson Anthology features the song "Farewell My Summer Love" in its 1984 remix, as well as "Don't Let it Get You Down", "Call on Me" and "To Make My Father Proud" in their original 1973 versions. All nine undubbed versions were released on Hello World: The Motown Solo Collection in June 2009.

TRACK LISTING 1. "Don't Let It Get You Down" Writer(s) Mel Larson, Jerry Marcellino, Deke Richards Length 3:02, "You've Really Got a Hold on Me" Writer(s) Smokey Robinson, White, Rogers Length 3:30, "Melodie" Writer(s) Mel Larson, Jerry Marcellino, Deke Richards Length 3:24 "Touch the One You Love" Writer(s) Wayne, Clinton Length 2:48 "Girl You're So Together" Length 3:12 " Farewell My Summer Love" Writer(s) Keni St. Lewis Length 3:12 "Call on Me" Writer(s) Fonce Mizell, Larry Mizell Length 3:39 "Here I Am (Come and Take Me)" Writer(s) Green, Hodges Length 2:56 To Make My Father Proud" Writer(s) Bob Crewe, Larry Weiss Length 4:04 **Bad** is the seventh studio album by American recording artist Michael Jackson. It was released on August 31, 1987 by Epic/CBS Records, nearly five years after his previous studio album, Thriller, which went on to become the world's best-selling album ever. Bad itself went on to sell over 32 million copies worldwide and shipped eight million units in the United States alone. It is the first, and currently only, album ever to feature five Billboard Hot 100 #1 singles. This album, Michael had even more freedom than he did with the two previous albums. Off the Wall and the world's best selling album of all time, Thriller, as he wrote and composed 9 of the album's 11 tracks, and co-wrote and produce another; "Man in the Mirror". The album, which saw the squeaky-clean pop idol adopt a street-tough image, continued his commercial success in the late '80s and won two Grammys. One for Best Music Video - Short Form for Leave Me Alone, and one for Best Engineered Album - Non Classical. Bad was ranked number 43 in the 100 Greatest Albums of All Time of the MTV Generation in 2009 by VH1. It was ranked number 202 in Rolling Stone magazine's 500 Greatest Albums of All Time. By the time Michael Jackson released this album, sales of its predecessor, Thriller, had already reached forty million, raising expectations for Bad. Bad became the first of his albums to debut at number one on the Billboard 200 where it remained for the next six consecutive weeks. The RIAA certified Bad for having sold eight million copies in the U.S. alone. In the U.K, the album sold 500,000 copies in just five days and is currently certified 13x platinum, for sales of 3.9 million, making it Michael's biggest-selling album in the UK. Globally, it is his overall third best-selling recording, behind Thriller and Dangerous, with 30 million copies sold. Michael Jackson set another record with this album, becoming the first, and currently only, artist to have five songs to hit number one from one album. In July 2006, it was announced by The Official UK Charts Company that Bad was the ninth biggest selling album in British history. It turned out to be the last collaborative effort by Michael Jackson and Quincy Jones. As Michael moved on to write and produce more of his own records, particularly with Teddy Riley, Rodney Jerkins, Jimmy Jam and Terry Lewis. Rolling Stone stated that "even without a milestone recording like "Billie Jean", Bad is still a better record than Thriller." The magazine further went on to say that the "filler" content in Bad - including songs such as "Speed Demon", "Dirty Diana" and "Liberian Girl" - is written by Michael Jackson himself, making Bad "richer, sexier and better than Thriller's forgettable."

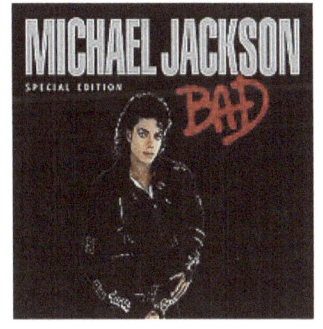

In 2001, a special edition of the album was released with three new songs and a new booklet containing lyrics and previously-unpublished photos. In 2003, the album was ranked number 202 on Rolling Stone magazine's list of the 500 greatest albums of all time. **TRACK LISTING** 1.

"Bad" Writer(s) Michael Jackson Length 4:07 2. "The Way You Make Me Feel" Writer(s) Michael Jackson Length 4:58 3. "Speed Demon" Writer(s) Michael Jackson Length 4:03 4. "Liberian Girl" Writer(s) Michael Jackson Length 3:53 5. "Just Good Friends" (duet with Stevie Wonder) Writer(s) Terry Britten, Graham Lyle Length 4:08 6. "Another Part of Me" Writer(s) Michael Jackson Length 3:54 7. "Mirror" Writer(s) Glen Ballard, Siedah Garrett Length 5:19 8. "I Just Can't Stop Loving You" (duet with Siedah Garrett) Writer(s) Michael Jackson Length 4:13 "Dirty Diana" Writer(s) Michael Jackson Length 4:41 "Smooth Criminal" Writer(s) Michael Jackson Length 4:17 "Leave Me Alone" Writer(s) Michael Jackson Length 4:40 Re-issues of Bad feature a number of changes when compared to the original 1987 release: "Bad" has a modified horn arrangement. "The Way You Make Me Feel" has richer vocalizations and background vocals. "I Just Can't Stop Loving You" omits Michael Jackson's spoken intro. "Dirty Diana" is replaced with the 7-inch edit of the song. "Smooth Criminal" omits the dramatic breathing within the intro. **DANGEROUS** - Epic - 11/26/1991 - DANGEROUS became his second album to debut at #1 on the Billboard 200 album chart, where it spent the next four consecutive weeks. In the space of 17 years, the record has sold over 32 million copies worldwide. This puts it second only to "THRILLER" as a commercial success. Includes: BLACK OR WHITE, HEAL THE WORLD, WILL YOU BE THERE, GONE TOO SOON, JAM. - **DANGEROUS Remember the Time** is a popular recording by rock, pop and R&B singer Michael Jackson in March of 1992. Released as the second single off Jackson's hit 1991 album, Dangerous, the song was a successful attempt by Jackson to create a New Jack swing-flavored R&B jam with co-producer Teddy Riley. The song hit #3 on the Billboard Hot 100 singles chart and #1 on Billboard's R&B Singles chart. In 1993, Michael Jackson gave a memorable performance of the song at the Soul Train Awards in a chair. This was because he had severely twisted his ankle as he was going into a spin during dance rehearsals the day before. Remember The Time received the Soul Train Award for Best Male R&B Single. The song was originally set to be a part of the Dangerous World Tour and was rehearsed before the tour began but was taken out. As with some of his past songs, the music video for "Remember the Time" (directed by John Singleton) was an elaborate production and became one of his longest videos at over 9 minutes. Set in ancient Egypt, it featured ground breaking visual effects and appearances by Eddie Murphy, Iman, Magic Johnson, and Tom "Tiny" Lister, Jr. along with a distinct physically complicated dance routine that became the centre piece of many other videos from the

Dangerous album and is one of only a few videos where he is seen embraced in a kiss. A double album called HIStory by Michael Jackson hits from hit from the past fifteen years **- Epic - 6/20/1995** -... The second, named "HIStory Continues" features new songs. With worldwide sales of 20 million (40 million in terms of units) it is the top grossing album of Jackson's career behind "THRILLER". It is Jackson's first album to have contained profanity. Includes: YOU ARE NOT ALONE, THEY DON'T CARE ABOUT US, SCREAM. - HIStory - STUDIO COMPILATION) - THE BEST OF MICHAEL JACKSON AND THE JACKSON 5 - Universal UK - (originally released in 1997) 10/22/01 - 20 Tracks - The early songs of Michael Jackson and also the Jackson 5 is all here. Includes: I WANT YOU BACK, ABC, THE LOVE YOU SAVE, I'LL BE THERE...many others. **BLOOD ON THE DANCE FLOOR-HIStory in the Mix** is a 1997 remix album by Michael Jackson. The album is made up of eight remixes from Michael Jackson's previous studio album HIStory, and five new songs. He was

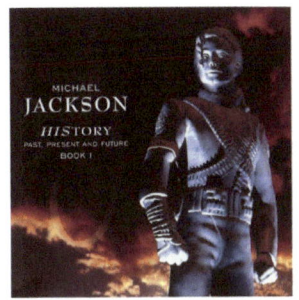
heavily involved with the production of the new material while the remixes were produced by other artists. The new material dealt with themes such as drug addiction, women and paranoia. The album received minimal promotion by Michael's standards, particularly in the US. Still, a film, two singles ("Blood on the Dance Floor" and "HIStory/Ghosts") and three music videos were issued as promotion. Reviews at the time of release were largely mixed; some critics felt that Michael Jackson had already explored these musical themes. Other critics were favorable, with praise issued for similarities to the music of Marilyn Manson and Trent Reznor. Worldwide sales stand at six million copies as of 2007, making it the best selling remix album ever released. Several contemporary critics view the material in an increasingly favorable light and believe the album could have been more successful. **JACKSON AND THE JACKSON 5-BLOOD ON THE DANCE FLOOR: HISTORY IN THE MIX** - Epic - 5/20/1997 - 13 Tracks - The album is made up of eight remixes from Jackson's previous studio album HIStory, and five new songs. The new material dealt with themes such as drug addiction, women and paranoia. The album received minimal promotion by Jackson's standards and reviews at the time of release were largely mixed. Worldwide sales stand at six million copies as of 2007, making it the best selling remix album ever released. Includes: BLOOD ON THE DANCE FLOOR, MORPHINE,

GHOST, STRANGER IN MOSCOW, EARTH SONG, YOU ARE NOT ALONE, HISTORY. - **TRACK LISTING** 1. "Blood on the Dance Floor" Writer(s) Michael Jackson, Teddy Riley Length 4:14 2. "Morphine" Writer(s) M. Jackson Length 6:26 3. "Superfly Sister" Writer(s) M. Jackson, Bryan Loren Length 6:27 4. "Ghosts" Writer(s) M. Jackson, Riley Length 5:13 5. "Is It Scary" Writer(s) M. Jackson, James Harris III, Terry Lewis Length 5:35 6. "Scream Louder (Flute Tyme Remix)" Writer(s) M. Jackson, Janet Jackson, Harris, Lewis Length 5:27 7. "Money (Fire Island Radio Edit)" Writer(s) M. Jackson Length 4:22 8. "2 Bad (Refugee Camp Mix)" Writer(s) M. Jackson, Bruce Swedien, Rene Austin, Dallas Austin Length 3:32 9. "Stranger in Moscow (Tee's In-House Club Mix)" Writer(s) M. Jackson Length 6:55 10. "This Time Around (D.M. Radio Mix)" M. Jackson, D. Austin Length 4:05 11. "Earth Song (Hani's Club Experience)" Writer(s) M. Jackson Length 7:55 12. "You Are Not Alone (Classic Club Mix)" Writer(s) R. Kelly Length 7:38 13. HIStory (Tony Moran's HIStory Lesson)" Writer(s) M. Jackson, Harris, Lewis Length 8:00 INVINCIBLE - *Epic - 10/30/2001 - 16 Tracks* - The tenth and final studio album completed and released by American recording artist Michael Jackson during his lifetime. When it was first released, it was available in five different colors - the standard silver cover, along with red, green, orange, and blue. As of 2009, the red, green, orange, and blue covers are out of print. To date, Invincible has sold around 10 million copies worldwide. **TRACK LISTING** 1. "Unbreakable" (Featuring The Notorious B.I.G.; background vocals by Brandy Norwood) Writer(s) Jackson, Daniels, Jerkis, Payne, Smith, Wallace Length 6:26, 2. "Heartbreaker" Writer(s) Jackson, Jerkins, Jerkins III, Daniels, Mischke, Gregg Length 5:09, 3. "Invincible" Writer(s) Jackson, Daniels, Gregg, Jerkins, Jerkins Length 4:46, 4. "Break of

Dawn" Writer(s) Jackson, Dr. Freeze Length 5:32, 5. "Heaven Can Wait" Writer(s) Jackson, Riley, Heard, Smith, Teron Beal, Laues, Quiller Length 4:49, 6. "You Rock My World" (Introductory skit featuring Chris Tucker) Writer(s) Jackson, Daniels, Jerkins, Jerkins, Payne Length 5:39 7."Butterflies" Writer(s) Harris, Ambrosius Length 4:40, 8. "Speechless" Writer(s) Jackson Length 3:18, 9. "2000 Watts" (Backing vocals by Teddy Riley) Writer(s) Jackson, Riley, Gibson, Henson Length 4:24, 10. "You Are My Life" Writer(s) Jackson, Babyface, Sager, McClain Length 4:33, 11. "Privacy" Writer(s) Jackson, Belle, Daniels, Jerkins, Jerkins Length 4:24, 12. "Don't Walk Away" Writer(s) Jackson, Riley, Stites, Vertelney Length 4:24, 13. "Cry" (also titled Cry (We Can Change The World) Writer(s) R. Kelly Length 5:00, 14. "The Lost

Children" Writer(s) Jackson Length 4:00, 15. "Whatever Happens" (Guitar by Carlos Santana) Writer(s) Jackson, Riley, Quay, Williams Length 4:56, 16. "Threatened" (Contains snippets of Rod Serling) Writer(s) Jackson, Jerkins, Jerkins III, Daniels, Length 4:18 NUMBER ONES - Epic - 11/18/2003 - 18 Tracks - It was Michael's first proper compilation album with Sony, after the release of HIStory – Past, Present and Future, Book I in 1995 (and after the re-release of that album as a single-CD, only-hits edition in 2001). The album included his singles that reportedly reached #1 in charts around the world (this way, the number-one rule was extended besides the UK/US-restricted politics used for the Beatles and Elvis compilations). Many other studios had released different compilations prior to this. Number Ones were successful around the world, reaching #1 in the UK and #13 in the United States. It proved to be an enduring catalog seller, eventually returning to the top spot in the UK charts on June 28, 2009 after his sudden death. It's sold more than 7.2 million copies worldwide to date. Includes: DON'T STOP TILL YOU GET ENOUGH, BILLIE JEAN, and THRILLER...many others. -NUMBER ONES-(STUDIO COMPILATION) - MICHAEL JACKSON: THE ULTIMATE COLLECTION - Legacy: Epic - 11/17/2004 - 57 Tracks (music) - 16 Track DVD - This is a limited-edition box set of Michael Jackson's music, consisting of four audio CDs and one DVD. Much of the music is drawn from the height of Jackson's career, particularly from the main five albums. The song "We've Had Enough" was written by Michael Jackson as a criticism of the Iraq War. The Collection box set also contains songs previously out of print. Includes: I want you back, P.Y.T and many others MICHAEL JACKSON THE ULTIMATE COLLECTION-(studio compilation) - THE ESSENTIAL MICHAEL JACKSON - Legacy: Epic - 7/19/2005 - 38 Tracks (U.S. version has 8 bonus tracks) - The Essential Michael Jackson is a 2005 greatest hits compilation released by Sony Music's catalog division. The compilation features thirty-eight hit songs by Michael Jackson, from his days at Motown Records with The Jackson 5 in the late 1970s to his 2001 hit "YOU ROCK MY WORLD". On August 26, 2008, The Essential Michael Jackson 3.0 was released in the US. In March 2009, the album reached new heights in the US, following Michael's announcement of new concerts. The set sold 102,000 units on the chart week ending July 1st 2009 following his death and would ultimately become the second biggest seller of the week behind his Number Ones compilation. Includes: I WANT YOU BACK, ABC, THE LOVE YOU SAVE, GOT TO BE THERE, WILL YOU BE THERE, DANGEROUS, YOU ARE

NOT ALONE, YOU ROCK MY WORLD, ...many others   -THE ESSENTIAL MICHAEL JACKSON- – THRILLER 25 - Legacy: Epic - 2/8/2008 - 17 Tracks, 4 DVD - Thriller 25 is a 25th Anniversary special edition reissue of the Michael Jackson album Thriller, the world's best selling album. Thriller 25 was released on CD and vinyl. It is the first Jackson album with an age certificate. Along with the original material, the reissue contained remixes, new material, a DVD and collaborations with several contemporary artists. Along with the original material there were seven bonus tracks. A new ballad called "For All Time"; the reissue was a commercial success, selling 3 million copies worldwide in 12 weeks and was generally well received among critics, despite their view that the new material was not as inspiring as the original. -THRILLER 25-- KING OF POP - Sony BMG, Epic - 8/22/2008 - King of Pop is a compilation album released in celebration of Michael Jackson's 50th birthday on August 29, 2008. Fans in each country

voted for the songs they wanted to be included in that nation's version of the album from a list of Jackson's back catalog. Aside from the tracks selected by fans, a mega-mix by Jason Nevins was also included. Each pool list and release date differed slightly according to nation. The album has been released in a total of 19 countries. There has been no announcement of a release date in the US. Currently the album has reached the top ten in the majority of countries it was released.-KING OF POP- 50 BEST SONGS: THE MOTOWN YEARS - Universal UK - 9/8/2008 - 50 Tracks - This 3 CD digipak release contains all of their hits throughout the Motown years from both the Jackson 5 ('ABC', 'I Want You Back', 'Never Can Say Goodbye') and Michael's solo material including 'You've Got A Friend', 'Ben', 'Ain't No Sunshine' and 'One Day In Your Life'. -50 BEST SONGS: THE MOTOWN YEARS-(LIVE ALBUM) - **ONE NIGHT IN JAPAN** - 101 Distribution - 7/14/2009 - 17 Tracks (2 Disc) - Pre-order offer. Includes: BEAT IT, BILLIE JEAN, SHAKE YOUR BODY, THILLIER. The Jackson 5 Ultimate Collection. A collection of songs of Michael and four his brothers...-The King Of Pop is showcased at his absolute best on this compilation of some of his very work of the 1980's and 1990's. This compendium of Michael greats mixes music videos, short films like "Moonwalker" and the full

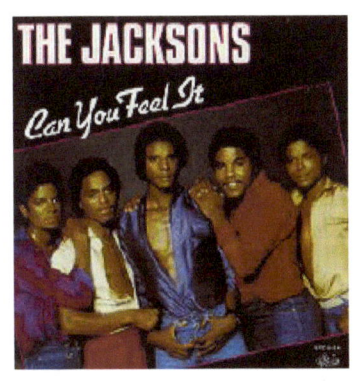

version "Thriller," and live performances, highlighting Michael's contributions to both the visual and live realms of pop music. TRIUMPH was a 1980 album by The Jacksons for CBS/Epic Records. A Platinum follow-up to the group's 1978 album, Destiny, the group shared lead vocals and special solo spots on all nine songs. Lead singer Michael Jackson handles most of the lead vocals himself. The album's hits included "LOVELY ONE", "CAN YOU FEEL IT" AND "HEARTBREAK HOTEL" (which was renamed "This Place Hotel" to avoid confusion with the Elvis Presley song of the same name). The album was a major success and the tour for this project is considered one of the best of the 1980s. "Can You Feel It" was a hit recording by funk and soul group The Jacksons, recorded in March 1980 and released in September 1980 as the first track on their album Triumph. Written by brothers Jackie and Michael, the song featured solo leads by Randy and Michael. Released as a single in 1981, the song reached #77 on the pop charts and number thirty on the R&B charts in United States, but reached number six in the UK and number two in The Netherlands in 1981. The accompanying video, directed by Bruce Gowers and Robert Abel, was noted for its remarkable special effects created by Robert Abel and Associates. In 2001, it was voted one of the 100 best videos of all time, in a poll to mark the 20th anniversary of MTV. The single was sampled by Tamperer featuring Maya for their 1998 dance hit "Feel It". It was also interpolated in the 2007 song "Carry Feelings" by South Rakkas Crew and T.O.K. The song again rose to prominence when in 2006, psycho-illusionist Derren Brown used the song along with various other psychological motivators to convince a group of 4 people to each commit a bank robbery by their own free will. When it was released, the album became The Jacksons' first album to reach number-one on the R&B Albums chart since MAYBE TOMORROW in 1971, and went Platinum a year after its release. The group would not release another studio LP for four years after Triumph's release. **TRACK LISTING** "Can You Feel It" (J. Jackson/M. Jackson) - 6:00 "Lovely One" (M. Jackson/R. Jackson) - 4:52 "Your Ways" (J. Jackson) - 4:31 "Everybody" (M. Jackson/T. Jackson/McKinney) - 5:00 "This Place Hotel" (M. Jackson) - 5:44 "Time Waits for No One" (J. Jackson/R. Jackson) - 3:24 "Walk Right Now" (M. Jackson/J. Jackson/R. Jackson) - 6:29 "Give It Up" (M. Jackson/R. Jackson) - 4:20 "Wondering Who" (J. Jackson/R. Jackson) - 4:19 "This Place Hotel" (Single Version)* - 4:52 " Walk Right Now" John Luongo Disco Mix) * - 7:36 "Walk Right Now" (John Luongo Instrumental Mix) * - 6:58 **LIVE IN**

BUCHAREST: The Dangerous Tour is a live concert DVD released by Michael Jackson in 2005. The DVD was previously included with the Michael Jackson: The Ultimate Collection box set. The concert took place during Michael's first leg on his Dangerous World Tour on October 1, 1992 at the Bucharest National Stadium, with a sold-out attendance of 70,000. This concert is the only concert by him that has been released on DVD; along with the HIStory Concert in Seoul, which was released as a VHS in Korea. The two concerts are the only ones that have been officially released. There are various versions of the same concert that exist. The first version was broadcasted the next day by BBC; following his death, this version was rebroadcast on BNN/Ned3. All the footage in this version is from the Bucharest concert. The version that appears on the DVD was broadcast on HBO in 1992, which became the highest audience in the channel's history for a single broadcast. This version, while mostly having footage of Michael Jackson performing at the Bucharest Concert, also consisted of many audience shots from concerts in other locations such as Madrid and Wembley, heavily edited crowd noises, and is also missing the We Are The World Interlude that was included in the original BBC Telecast, leading to some criticism from some fans. The DVD has sold 950,000 copies worldwide. **Dangerous** is the eighth album by Michael Jackson, released on November 26, 1991. It became his second to debut at #1 on the Billboard 200 album chart, where it spent the next four consecutive weeks. In the space of 17 years, media sources state the record has sold as much as 32 million copies worldwide, with 7 million certified shipments in the United States alone, making it a faster selling album than his previous record Bad. The album won one Grammy for Best Engineered Album - Non Classical won by Bruce Swedien & Teddy Riley[2] and is the most successful New Jack Swing album of all time.[3]. Dangerous was the first album ever to spawn eight consecutive UK Top 20 hits. "Dangerous" was Michael Jackson's second best-selling album (first was Thriller). According to the sleeve notes on the later remastered edition of the album, recording sessions began in Los Angeles, California at Ocean Way/Record One Studio 2 on June 25, 1990. The sessions ended at Larrabee North and Ocean Way Studio on October 29, 1991, being the most extensive recording project of his career at the time (over 16 months compared to the usual 6 spent for his previous three studio albums). In March 1991, Michael signed a 15 year, 6 album deal to Sony

Music. The press reported that Sony actually handed over $1 billion to him, but that was not the case. At the time, Sony estimated that if the albums he released under the new contract sold at the same level they currently sold, it would generate over $1 billion in profits for them. Additionally, Michael was awarded the highest royalty rate in the business. By the time the contract expired in March 2006, Michael would have been paid $45 million from Sony ($1 million a year, plus $5 million per album delivered). This does not include money he would have also earned from sales of albums, singles, videos etc. Under this contract, he is estimated to have

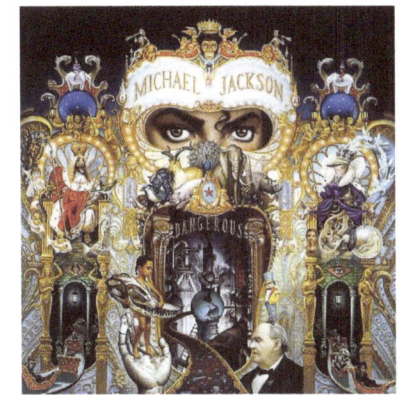

earned $175 million from album sales alone. At this point, Dangerous was already in the making, under the producing talents of (Quincy Jones recommended) 22 year old New Jack Swing inventor Teddy Riley and Grammy-winner Bill Bottrell. The previous album, Bad, was Michael's last designed for the LP industry, conforming to the usual 10-song within 50-minute format, whereas Dangerous was a 77-minute, 14-track compilation, which almost dared the capacity of early Nineties compact discs. Consequently, the record was released as a double album in vinyl. The album was initially released in a large box with a picture of his eyes, which folded open to reveal the normal cover (painted by pop surrealist Mark Ryden), in pop-up card, with the CD and booklet in the bottom. Dangerous was a highly anticipated album, as shown by an incident at the Los Angeles International Airport, where a group of armed robbers stole 30,000 copies before its official release.[4] The Album also spawned a worldwide concert tour, The Dangerous Tour. American Music Awards: Best Pop/Rock Album, "Dangerous" **TRACK LISTING** 1. "Jam" Writer(s) René Moore, Bruce Swedien, Michael Jackson, Teddy Riley Length 5:39 2. "Why You Wanna Trip on Me" Writer(s) Riley, Bernard Belle Length 5:24 3. "In the Closet" Writer(s) Jackson, Riley, rap lyrics by Vashawn Length 6:31 4. "She Drives Me Wild" Writer(s) Jackson, Riley, rap lyrics by Aquil Davidson Length 3:41 5. "Remember the Time" Writer(s) Riley, Jackson, Belle Length 4:00 6. "Can't Let Her Get Away" Writer(s) Jackson, Riley Length 4:58 7. "Heal the World" Writer(s) Jackson Length 6:24 8. "Black or White" (feat. Slash on guitar) Writer(s) Jackson, rap lyrics by Bill Bottrell Length 4:15 9. "Who Is It" Writer(s) Jackson Length 6:34 10. "Give In to Me" (feat. Slash on guitar) Writer(s) Jackson, Bottrell Length 5:29 11. "Will You Be There" Writer(s) Jackson Length 7:40 12. "Keep The Faith" Writer(s) Glen Ballard, Siedah Garrett,

Jackson Length 5:57 13. "Gone Too Soon" Writer(s) Larry Grossman, Buz Kohan Length 3:26 14. "Dangerous" Writer(s) Jackson, Bottrell, Riley Length 6:59

Michael Jackson Singles "Got to Be There" · "Rockin' Robin" · "I Wanna Be Where You Are" · "Ain't No Sunshine" · "Ben" · "With a Child's Heart" · "Happy" · "We're Almost There" · "Just a Little Bit of You" · "Ease on Down the Road" · "You Can't Win" · "Don't Stop 'til You Get Enough" · "Rock with You" · "Off the Wall" · "She's Out of My Life" · "Girlfriend" · "The Girl Is Mine" · "Billie Jean" · "Beat It" · "Wanna Be Startin' Somethin'" · "Human Nature" · "P.Y.T. (Pretty Young Thing)" · "Thriller" · "One Day in Your Life" · "The Girl Is Mine" · "Billie Jean" · "Beat It" · · "I Just Can't Stop Loving You" · "Bad" · "The Way You Make Me Feel" · "Man in the Mirror" · "Dirty Diana" · "Another Part of Me" · "Smooth Criminal" · "Leave Me Alone" · "Liberian Girl" · "Black or White" · **"Remember the Time"** · "In the Closet" · "Jam" · "Who Is It" · "Give In to Me" · "Heal the World" · "Will You Be There" · "Gone Too Soon" · "Scream/Childhood" · "You Are Not Alone" · "Earth Song" · "They Don't Care About Us" · "Stranger in Moscow" · "Blood on the Dance Floor" · "HIStory/Ghosts" · "You Rock My World" · "Cry" · **"Butterflies"** · "One More Chance" · "The Girl Is Mine 2008" · "Wanna Be Startin' Somethin' 2008" · "Say Say Say" · "Somebody's Watching Me" · "Tell Me I'm Not Dreamin'" · "We Are the World" · "Get It" · "Dangerous" · "D.S." · "Why" · "I Need You" · "What More Can I Give" · "Do the Bartman"

"The publication described Michael Jackson's influence at that point as, "Star of records, radio, rock video. A one-man rescue team for the music business. A songwriter who sets the beat for a decade. A dancer with the fanciest feet on the street. A singer who cuts across all boundaries of taste and style and color too"

THRILLER

"IN A CLASS ALL BY ITSELF"

Thriller is the sixth studio album by American recording artist Michael Jackson. The album was released on November 30, 1982 by Epic Records as the follow-up to his successful 1979 album Off the Wall. Thriller explores similar genres to those of Off the Wall, including funk, disco, soul, soft rock, R&B, and pop. Thriller's lyrics deal with themes including paranoia and the supernatural. With a production budget of $750,000, recording sessions took place between April and November 1982 at Westlake Recording Studios in Los Angeles, California.[9] Assisted by producer Quincy Jones, he wrote four of Thriller's nine tracks. Following the release of the album's first single "The Girl Is Mine", some observers assumed Thriller would only be a minor hit record. With the release of the second single "Billie Jean", the album topped the charts in many countries. At its peak, the album was selling a million copies a week worldwide. In just over a year, Thriller became-and currently remains-the best-selling album of all time. Sales are estimated to be over 110 million copies sold worldwide.[10] Seven of the album's nine songs were released as singles, and all reached the top 10 on the Billboard Hot 100. The album won a record-breaking eight Grammy Awards at the 1984 Grammys. Thriller cemented Michael Jackson's status as one of the predominant pop stars of the late 20th century, and enabled him to break down racial barriers via his appearances on MTV and meetings with President Ronald Reagan at the White House. The album was one of the first to use music videos as successful promotional tools-the videos for "Thriller", "Billie Jean" and "Beat It" all received regular rotation on MTV.

In 2001, a special edition issue of the album was released, which contains additional audio interviews, a demo recording and the song "Someone In the Dark", which was a Grammy-winning track from the E.T. the Extra-Terrestrial storybook.[11]

In 2008, the album was reissued again as Thriller 25, containing re-mixes that feature contemporary artists, a previously unreleased song and a DVD. Thriller ranked number 20 on Rolling Stone magazine's 500 Greatest Albums of All Time list in 2003, and was listed by the

National Association of Recording Merchandisers at number three in its Definitive 200 Albums of All Time. Thriller was preserved by the Library of Congress to the National Recording Registry, as it was deemed "culturally significant". Michael reunited with Off the Wall producer Quincy Jones to record his sixth studio album. The pair worked together on 300 songs, nine of which were eventually included.[19] Thriller was recorded between April and November 1982, with a production budget of $750,000. Several members of the band Toto were also involved in the album's recording and production.[19] Michael wrote four songs for the record: "Wanna Be Startin' Somethin'", "The Girl Is Mine" (with Paul McCartney), "Beat It" and "Billie Jean".[20]

Unlike many artists, he did not write these songs on paper. Instead, he would dictate into a sound recorder; when recording he would sing from memory.[21][22] Michael spent much of his time rehearsing dance steps alone.[22] When the album's nine songs were completed, both Quincy and Michael were unhappy with the result and remixed every song, spending a week on each.[22] Quincy believed that "Billie Jean" was not strong enough to be included on the record, but Michael disagreed and kept it. Quincy Jones told Michael Jackson that Thriller would be unlikely to sell successfully like Off the Wall had, because the market had since weakened. In response, Michael threatened to cancel the album's release.[19] Michael was inspired to create an album where "every song was a killer," as with Tchaikovsky's The Nutcracker, and developed Thriller on that concept.[23][24] Quincy Jones and songwriter Rod Temperton gave detailed accounts of what occurred for the 2001 reissue of the album. Quincy discussed "Billie Jean" and why it was so personal to Michael, who struggled to deal with a number of obsessed fans. Quincy Jones wanted the long introduction on the song to be shortened; however, Michael insisted that it remain because it made him want to dance.[20] The ongoing backlash against disco made it necessary to move in a different musical direction from the disco-heavy Off the Wall.[24] Quincy and Michael were determined to make a rock song that would appeal to all tastes and spent weeks looking for a suitable guitarist for the song "Beat It", a song Michael wrote and played drums on. Eventually, they found Eddie Van Halen of the rock band Van Halen.[20][22] When Rod Temperton wrote the song "Thriller", he originally wanted to call it "Starlight" or "Midnight Man" but settled on "Thriller" because he felt the name had merchandising potential.[22] Always wanting a notable person to recite the closing lyrics, Temperton brought in actor Vincent Price, who completed his part in just two takes. Temperton wrote the spoken portion in a taxi on the way to the recording studio. Jones and Temperton said that some recordings were left off the final cut because they did not have the "edginess" of other album tracks. According to Steve Huey of Allmusic, Thriller refined the strengths of Michael's previous album Off the Wall; the dance and rock tracks were more aggressive, while the pop tunes and ballads were softer and more soulful.[26]

Notable tracks include the ballads "The Lady in My Life", "Human Nature", and "The Girl Is Mine"; the funk pieces "Billie Jean" and "Wanna Be Startin' Somethin'"; and the disco set "Baby Be Mine" and "P.Y.T. (Pretty Young Thing)".[1][5][6][26] "Wanna Be Startin' Somethin'" was written a few years prior to 1982 and has a similar sound to the material on Off The Wall. The song is accompanied by a bass and percussion background and the song's centerpiece, a climaxing Swahili chant, gave the song an international flavor.[27] "The Girl Is Mine" tells of two friends' fight over a woman, arguing over who loves her more and concludes with a spoken rap.[22][27] Despite the light pop flavor of these two records, Thriller, more so than Off the Wall, displayed foreshadowing of the contradictory thematic elements that would come to characterize Michael's later work.[28] With Thriller, Michael Jackson would begin his association with the subliminal theme of paranoia and darker imagery.[5] This is evident on the songs "Billie Jean", "Wanna Be Startin' Somethin'" and "Thriller".[1] In "Billie Jean", Michael sings about an obsessive fan who alleges he has fathered a child of hers; in "Wanna Be Startin' Somethin'" he argues against gossips and the media.[5][26] In the former song, Quincy had him sing vocal overdubs through a six-foot-long cardboard tube, and brought in jazz saxophonist Tom Scott to play a rare instrument, the lyricon, a wind-controlled analog synthesizer. Bassist Louis Johnson ran through his part on a Yamaha bass guitar. The song opens with a long bass-and-drums introduction.[29] In the song "Thriller", sound effects such as creaking door, thunder, feet walking on wooden planks, winds and howling dogs can be heard.[22] The anti-gang-violence "Beat It" became a homage to West Side Story, and was Michael's first successful rock cross-over piece.[26][30] Michael later said of "Beat It", "the point is no one has to be the tough guy, you can walk away from a fight and still be a man. You don't have to die to prove you're a man".[27] "Human Nature" is moody and introspective, as conveyed in lyrics such as, "Looking out, across the morning, the City's heart begins to beat, reaching out, I touch her shoulder, I'm dreaming of the street".[27] By the late 1970s, Michael's abilities as a vocalist were well regarded; Allmusic described him as a "blindingly gifted vocalist".[12] Rolling Stone compared his vocals to the "breathless, dreamy stutter" of Stevie Wonder. Their analysis was also that "Jackson's feathery-timbre tenor is extraordinary beautiful. It slides smoothly into a startling falsetto that's used very daringly".[13] With the release of Thriller, Michael Jackson could sing low-down to a basso low C-

but he preferred to sing higher because pop tenors have more range to create style.[31] Rolling Stone were of the opinion that Michael Jackson was now singing in a "fully adult voice" that was "tinged by sadness".[5] "P.Y.T. (Pretty Young Thing)", credited to James Ingram and Quincy Jones, and "Lady in My Life" by Rod Temperton, both gave the album a stronger R&B direction; the latter song was described as "the closest Jackson has come to crooning a sexy, soulful ballad after his Motown years" by Taraborrelli.[27] The singer had already adopted a "vocal hiccup" which he continued to implement in Thriller. The purpose of the hiccup-somewhat like a gulping for air or gasping-is to help promote a certain emotion; be it excitement, sadness or fear.[32] Thriller was released on November 30, 1982, and sold one million copies worldwide per week at its peak.[31] Seven singles were released "The Girl Is Mine" was followed by the hit single "Billie Jean", which made Thriller a chart-topper.[33][34] Success continued with the single "Beat It", which featured guitarists Eddie Van Halen and Steve

Lukather.[35] The title track "Thriller" was released as a single and also became a hit internationally.[27] Thriller was mostly well received by critics. A four-star Rolling Stone review by Christopher Connelly described it as "a zesty LP" with a "harrowing, dark message". Despite the positive response, the title track came under strong criticism. The New York Times gave a positive review of the album, and dedicated a large amount of its coverage to the song "Human Nature". They described it as the most "striking" song on the record, and wrote, "This is a haunting, brooding ballad by Steve Porcaro and John Bettis with an irresistible chorus and it should be an enormous hit". Concluding their review The New York Times added; "there are other hits here, too, lots of them. Best of all, with a pervasive confidence infusing the album as a whole, Thriller suggests that Mr. Jackson's evolution as an artist is far from finished".[8] Robert Christgau published a positive (A-) graded overview of the album a few days before its release. He acknowledged that there were "fillers" on the record but still labeled it "almost classic. A year after the album's release, Time summed up the three main singles from the album, saying, "The pulse of America and much of the rest of the world moves irregularly, beating in time to the tough strut of "Billie Jean", the asphalt aria of "Beat It", the supremely cool chills of "Thriller".[31] The album won Michael Jackson a record-breaking seven Grammy Awards in 1984, including Album of the Year. The eighth Grammy went to Bruce Swedien.[36][37] That same year, he won eight American Music Awards, the Special Award of Merit and three MTV Video Music Awards.[38] Thriller was recognized as the world's best-selling album on February 7, 1984, when it was inducted into the Guinness Book of World Records.[39] It is one of only three albums to remain in the top ten of the Billboard 200 for a full year, and spent 37 weeks at number one out of the 80 consecutive weeks it was in the top ten. The album was also the first of three to have seven Billboard Hot 100 top ten singles, and was the only album to be the best-seller of two years (1983–1984) in the US.[40][41] In February 2008, Epic Records released Thriller 25; Michael served as executive producer.[43] Thriller 25 appeared on CD, USB and vinyl with seven bonus tracks, a new song called "For All Time", Vincent Price's voice-over, and five re-mixes featuring American artists Fergie, will.i.am, Kanye West, and Akon.[43]

On March 6, 2009 Thriller was certified 28x Platinum by the Recording Industry Association of America, for shipments of at least 28 million copies in the US giving it Double Diamond Award status there.[42][43] The album topped the charts in many countries, sold 3.7 million copies in the UK,[43][44] 2.5 million in Japan[45] and went 14x Platinum in Australia.[46] Still popular today, Thriller sells an estimated 130,000 copies in the US per year; it reached number two in the US Catalog charts in February 2003 and number 39 in the UK in March 2007.[38] The album is cited as having sold between 47 and 110 million copies worldwide; the Guinness Book of World Records lists Thriller as having sold 65 million copies as of 2007. Blender described Michael Jackson as the "late twentieth century pre-eminent pop icon", while The New York Times gave the opinion that he was a "musical phenomenon", and that "in the world of pop music, there is Michael Jackson and there is everybody else".[29][52] Michael Jackson changed the way the industry functioned: both as an artistic persona, and as a financial, profitable entity. His attorney John Branca observed that Michael achieved the highest royalty rate in the music industry to that point: approximately $2 for each album sold. As a result, Jackson earned record-breaking profits from compact disc sales, and from the sale of copies of the documentary, The Making of Michael Jackson's Thriller, produced by Michael Jackson and John Landis. Funded by MTV, the film sold over 350,000 copies in its first few months. In a market then driven by singles, Thriller raised the significance of albums, yet its multiple hit singles changed perceived notions as to the number of successful singles that could be taken from an individual album.[53] The era saw the arrival of novelties like the Michael Jackson doll that appeared in stores in May 1984 at a price of $12.[31] Thriller retains a position in American culture; biographer J. Randy Taraborrelli explains, "At some point, Thriller stopped selling like a leisure item—like a magazine, a toy, tickets to a hit movie-and started selling like a household staple".[54] At the time of the album's release, a press statement from Gil Friesen, the then President of A&M Records, read that, "The whole industry has a stake in this success".[31] Time magazine speculated that "the fallout from Thriller has given the [music] business its best years since the heady days of 1978, when it had an estimated total domestic revenue of $4.1 billion".[31] Time summed up Thriller's impact as a "restoration of confidence" for an industry bordering on "the ruins of punk and the chic regions of synthesizer pop". The publication described Michael Jackson's influence at that point as, "Star of records, radio, rock video. A one-man rescue team for the music business. A songwriter who sets the beat for a decade. A dancer with the fanciest feet on the street. A singer who cuts across all boundaries of taste and style and color too".[31] Before the success of Thriller, many felt Michael Jackson had struggled to get MTV airing because he was black.[29] In an effort to attain air time for Michael, CBS Records President Walter Yetnikoff pressured MTV and declared, "I'm not going to give you any more videos and I'm going to go public and tell them about the fact you don't want to play music by a black guy".[29] His position persuaded MTV to begin airing "Billie Jean" and later "Beat It", which led to a long partnership and later helped other black music artists to gain mainstream recognition.[55] MTV denies claims of racism in their broadcasting.[56] The popularity of his videos, such as "Beat It" and "Billie Jean", helped to place the young channel "on the map", and MTV's focus shifted in favor of pop and R&B.[55][57] Michael Jackson in the revolutionary Thriller video. He transformed the medium of music video into an art form and promotional tool through the use of complex story lines, dance routines, special effects and cameo appearances by well known personalities.[26] When the 14-minute-long Thriller video aired, MTV ran it twice an hour to meet demand.[58] The short film marked an increase in scale for music videos and has been routinely named the best music video ever.[53] The popularity of the video sent the album back to number one in the album chart, but Michael's label did not support the release of the third music video from the album. They were already pleased with its success, so Michael convinced MTV to fund the project.[22][58] Author, music critic and journalist

Nelson George wrote in 2004, "It's difficult to hear the songs from Thriller and disengage them from the videos. For most of us the images define the songs. In fact, it could be argued that Michael is the first artist of the MTV age to have an entire album so intimately connected in the public imagination with its imagery". Short films like Thriller largely remained unique to Michael  Jackson, while the group dance sequence in "Beat It" has been frequently imitated. The choreography in Thriller has become a part of global pop culture, replicated everywhere from Bollywood to prisons in the Philippines. For a black artist in the 1980s to that point, his success was unprecedented. According to The Washington Post, Thriller paved the way for other African-American artists such as Prince. "The Girl Is Mine" was credited for getting interracial love on the radio. Time noted, "Jackson is the biggest thing since The Beatles. He is the hottest single phenomenon since Elvis Presley. He just may be the most popular black singer ever". A Michael Jackson celebrity impersonator for the 25th anniversary of the album Thriller at the 2008 Tribeca Film Festival with performers from Step It Up and Dance. Today, the album is still viewed in a positive light by critics some two decades later. Stephen Thomas Erlewine of Allmusic gave the album the maximum five stars, and wrote that the record had something to interest everyone. He believed it showcased harder funk and hard rock while remaining "undeniably fun". He went on to compliment "Billie Jean" and "Wanna Be Startin' Somethin'" and said, "The record's two best songs: 'Billie Jean ...and the delirious 'Wanna Be Startin' Somethin'', the freshest funk on the album [but] the most claustrophobic, scariest track Michael Jackson ever recorded." Erlewine gave the opinion that it was an improvement on the artist's previous album. Slant Magazine gave the album five stars and the Rolling Stone review, paid a compliment to the lyrics of "Wanna Be Startin' Somethin'".[6] The author Nelson George wrote that Jackson "has educated R. Kelly, Usher, Justin Timberlake and countless others with Thriller as a textbook".[63] As a sign of the album's longevity, in 2003 Thriller was ranked at number 20 on the Rolling Stone 500 Greatest Albums of All Time list, and was listed by the National Association of Recording Merchandisers at number three of the Definitive 200 Albums of All Time.[64][65]

In 2008, 25 years after its release, the record was inducted into the Grammy Hall of Fame and, a few weeks later, was among 25 recordings preserved by the Library of Congress to the National Recording Registry as "culturally significant".[66][67]

In 2009, music critics for MTV Base and VH1 both listed Thriller as the best album released since 1981.[68] Thriller, along with other critic favorites were then polled by the public. 40,000 people found Thriller to be the Best Album of all time by MTV Generation, gaining a third of all votes.[68][69] Thriller was reissued in 2001 in an expanded set titled Thriller: Special Edition. The original tracks were re-mastered, and the album included a new booklet and bonus material, including the songs "Someone in the Dark", "Carousel", and Jackson's original "Billie Jean" demo, as well as audio interviews with Jones and Temperton discussing the recording of the album.[20][70] Sony also hired sound engineer and mixer Mick Guzauski [71][72] to work with Michael on creating 5.1-channel surround sound mixes of Thriller, as well as all his other albums, for release on the then-new Super Audio CD format. Despite numerous retries, the artist never approved any of the mixes.[73] Consequently, Thriller was issued on SACD with the stereo mix only. [74][75] It also included a DVD featuring three music videos, the Motown 25 "Billie Jean" performance, and a booklet with a message from Michael Jackson.[43] The ballad "For All Time" supposedly dates from 1982, but is often credited as being from Dangerous sessions.[76] Two singles were released from the reissue: "The Girl Is Mine 2008" and "Wanna Be Startin' Somethin' 2008". Thriller 25 was a commercial success and did particularly well as a reissue. It peaked at number one in eight countries and Europe. It peaked at number two in the US, number three in the UK and reached the top 10 in over 30 national charts. It was certified Gold in 11 countries including the UK, received a 2x Gold certification in France and received platinum certification in Poland.[77][78][79] In the United States, Thriller 25 was the second best-selling album of its release week, selling one hundred and sixty six thousand copies, just fourteen thousand short of reaching the number one position. It was ineligible for the Billboard 200 chart as a re-release but entered the Pop Catalog Charts at number one (where it stayed for ten non-consecutive weeks),[80] with the best sales on that chart since December, 1996.[81][82][83] With the arrival of Halloween that November, Thriller 25 spent an eleventh non-consecutive week atop the US catalog chart. This brought US sales of the album to 688,000 copies, making it the best selling catalog album of 2008.[84] This was Michael Jackson's best launch since Invincible in 2001, selling three million copies worldwide in 12 weeks.[85] After Michael Jackson's death in June 2009, Thriller set additional records. It sold more than 100,000 copies, placing it at number two on the Top Pop Catalog Albums chart. Songs from Thriller also helped Michael Jackson become the first artist to sell more than one million song downloads in a week. All songs written and composed by the Michael Jackson, except where noted. **TRACK LISTING** 1. Title "Wanna Be

Startin' Somethin'" Length 6:02 2. Title "Baby Be Mine" (Rod Temperton) Length 4:20 3. Title "The Girl Is Mine" (with Paul McCartney) Length 3:42 4. Title "Thriller" (Temperton) Length 5:57 5. Title "Beat It" Length 4:17 6. Title "Billie Jean" Length 4:54 7. Title "Human Nature" (John Bettis, Steve Porcaro) 4:05 8. Title "P.Y.T. (Pretty Young Thing)" (James Ingram, Quincy Jones) Length 3:58 9. Title "The Lady in My Life" (Temperton) Length 4:59

Genre/Length	R&B, dance, dance-pop, pop/rock, funk/42:19
Label	Epic EK-38112
Producer	Michael Jackson and Quincy Jones

Michael Jackson Chronology		
Off the Wall	**Thriller**	Bad
(1979)	**(1982)**	(1987)

Thriller 25 (Live recording, from the 1981 album The Jacksons: Live Thriller 25 is the 25th Anniversary special edition reissue of the Michael Jackson album Thriller, the world's best selling album. The prospect of a "second chapter" to Thriller was first publicly discussed on Access Hollywood in late 2006. Jackson said he would discuss the idea with collaborator Will.i.am. It was released in Australia on February 8, 2008, then internationally on February 11, 2008 and the following day in the United States.[3] Thriller 25 was released by Sony BMG's re-issue division, Legacy Recordings. In the United Kingdom, the BBFC gave it a '15' Certificate because it included the "Thriller" music video. It is the first Jackson album with an age certificate. Along with the original material, the reissue contained remixes, new material, a DVD and collaborations with several contemporary artists. Two singles, "The Girl Is Mine 2008" and "Wanna Be Startin' Somethin' 2008" were released from the album to moderate success and a number of the other remixes charted, despite no physical release. The reissue was a commercial success, selling 3 million copies worldwide in 12 weeks and was generally well received among critics, despite their view that the new material was not as inspiring as the original. **TRACK LISTING** 1."Wanna Be Startin' Somethin'" 2. "Baby Be Mine" 3. "The Girl Is Mine" (with Paul McCartney) 4. "Thriller" 5. "Beat It" 6. "Billie Jean" 7. "Human Nature" 8. "P.Y.T. (Pretty Young Thing)" 9. "The Lady In My Life" 10."Voice-over

Session from "Thriller" Vincent Price (Temperton) - 0:24 11."The Girl Is Mine 2008" with Will.i.am (Jackson/Will.i.am/Harris) - 3:11 12."P.Y.T. (Pretty Young Thing) 2008" with Will.i.am (Jackson/Will.i.am/Harris) - 4:21 13. "Wanna Be Startin' Somethin' 2008" with Akon (Jackson/Akon/Tuinfort) - 4:14 14. "Beat It 2008" with Fergie (Jackson) - 4:12 15. "Billie Jean 2008" Kanye West Remix" (Jackson) - 4:37 16. "For All Time" (Sherwood/Porcaro) - 4:03 17. "Got the Hots" (Jackson/Jones) - 4:27 (Released only in Japan) DVD 1."Billie Jean" 2."Beat It" 3. "Thriller" 4. "Billie Jean" (live, Motown 25)[13] Thriller 25: Japanese Single Collection (Japanese exclusive) In 2008 a limited edition of Thriller 25 was released in Japan. [14] CD 1 "The Girl Is Mine" 2. "Can't Get Outta the Rain" CD 2 "Billie Jean" 2. "It's the Falling in Love" CD 3 "Beat It" "Get on the Floor" CD 4 "Wanna Be Startin' Somethin'" "Wanna Be Startin' Somethin'" (Instrumental) CD 5 "Human Nature" "Baby Be Mine" CD 6 "P.Y.T. (Pretty Young Thing)" "Working Day and Night" (Live recording, from the 1981 album The Jacksons: Live) CD 7 "Thriller" "Things I Do for You" (Live recording, from the 1981 album The Jacksons: Live

MICHAEL JACKSON ON THE COVER

FANS REACTIONS

His death triggered an outpouring of grief. Fans gathered outside the UCLA Medical Center, his Holmby Hills home, the Apollo Theater in New York, and at Hitsville U.S.A., the old Motown headquarters in Detroit where his career began, now the Motown Museum. Streets around the hospital were blocked off, and across America people left offices and factories to watch the breaking news on television.

Upon his death, many fans left remembrances at the Hollywood star, located at 1541 Vine Street, awarded to a long time radio talk show host also named Michael Jackson. Upon hearing of this, the radio commentator said, "I am willingly loan it to him and, if it would bring him back, he can have it. He was a real star. Sinatra, Presley, the Beatles and Michael Jackson" U.S. President Barack Obama sent a letter of condolence to the Jackson family, and during a press conference the Press Secretary Robert Gibbs said that President Obama viewed Jackson as a "spectacular performer, and a music icon". In Congress, Representatives Diane Watson and Jesse Jackson Jr. asked members to observe a moment of silence. Celebrities provided varied comments. Madonna and Diana Ross released statements saying they could not stop crying. Jackson's former wife, Lisa Marie Presley, said the singer had told her he was afraid he would end up like Elvis Presley, her father. Elizabeth Taylor, a long-time friend, said she can't imagine life without him." Liza Minnelli told CBS, "When the autopsy comes, all hell's going to break loose, so thank God we're celebrating him now." Jamie Foxx stated: "We want to celebrate this black man. He belongs to us and we shared him with everybody else."

Comment ~ Aisha-"Michael Jackson captured my heart the minute I heard him. I don't remember me reciting many other songs besides Michael Jackson. He was all I watched besides Barney. I can always listen to Michael Jackson song like it's the first time I ever heard it. He's was a genius and he will always be my favorite."

Comment ~ Anelda aka JazzyKitty- "I have been a fan of Michael all my life, the earliest I can remember is about 6 years old. I remember being in the fan club with my Aunt Linda, receiving a letter and a heart sticker with his face on it. I am devastated by this lost but I know God doesn't make mistakes. I am grateful that I could publish this book as a tribute to him because I truly lost a part of me. It is really hard for me to describe how I feel. I hope the book and the poem sums it up. May Mike get the peace now that he deserves!"

Comment ~ Guinness World Records Remembers Michael Jackson-Guinness World Records was saddened to hear of the death of Michael Jackson at the age of 50. Speaking in London tonight, Guinness World Records Editor-in-Chief, Craig Glenday commented "I will always be immensely proud to know that Michael considered me a friend, and I know that everyone at Guinness World Records will be numb from hearing the news that this gentle, kind, shy man is no longer with us. On his last visit to the Guinness World Records office, he devoted a few valuable hours of his time being photographed with everyone, and we were all touched by his humility and willingness to please everyone present with autographs and photos. I'm honored to have had the chance to spend some time with such a wonderfully talented artist - the man we called the Most Famous Living Man on Earth - and to present him with his favorite world record of all, the biggest selling album of all time, for Thriller, of course. He leaves behind an incredible musical legacy and a body of work unrivalled by any other performer."

Comment ~ Guinness World Records Editor-in-Chief, Craig Glenday- "I will always be immensely proud to know that Michael considered me a friend, and I know that everyone at Guinness World Records will be numb from hearing the news that this gentle, kind, shy man is no longer with us. On his last visit to the Guinness World Records office, he devoted a few valuable hours of his time being photographed with everyone, and we were all touched by his humility and willingness to please everyone present with autographs and photos. I'm honored to have had the chance to spend some time with such a wonderfully talented artist - the man we called the Most Famous Living Man on Earth - and to present him with his favorite world record of all, the biggest selling album of all time, for Thriller, of course. He leaves behind an incredible musical legacy and a body of work unrivalled by any other performer."

Comment ~ Katrina a member from Issecolor Sent Jun 26-"Thanks pretty girl! I am taking this hard...I never met him so I feel silly that it's bothering me like this. If feel this way, I know his family must be in an awful state of mind right now. We'll keep them in our prayers... Thanks for checking in Chica." :)

Comment ~ Mo-"When I heard the news I just felt bad for my mom Anelda so I kept calling her because I knew she was really sad that Michael had died. I loved him too. I always tried to dance like him. Also, I thought my mom was his biggest fan of MJ but I don't know because I see Ms. T wearing his button everyday. Mike was the bomb and he will be missed.

Comment ~ Terri Pope-My First Lady loves Michael, when I was at her house at for

Fellowship she had his videos on the entire day. She loves to say "Hee Hee" she also told us how Michael touched her life while growing up.

Comment ~ Marquita T. Scott-"I was in the supermarket when I heard the news and I was shocked. My family and I have been MJ fans all our lives. He will be missed. R.I.P., MJ."

Comment ~ Ryan White's Mom Remembers Michael Jackson-The mother of Ryan White, a hemophiliac teenager who died of AIDS-related illness in 1990 after contracting HIV through a blood transfusion, mourns the loss of music icon Michael Jackson, who died from cardiac arrest on June 25, FOX 35 reports. Michael befriended the teen in the late 1980s and, after Ryan's death, dedicated a song to him titled "Gone Too Soon." Jeanne White remembers Michael as a good-hearted person. "He worked so hard ever since he was a kid that he didn't have a childhood, and when you went to Neverland [Michael Jackson's former home], you too would act as a kid," she said.

Comment ~ Linda Roberts-"Okay! Well initially when I heard the news that Michael had went into cardiac arrest I really didn't believe it and when the reports came in to say that in fact he had passed, I had to hear it from a reliable source. So when CNN reported that yes he passed, I guess like millions of others I went into shock. I was at home and on my way to Wal-Mart so at the store, I purchased a Best of CD and I started asking strangers "Did you hear Michael Jackson died?" Probably wishing they would tell me the reports were false. In the days to follow I would wake up and in the forefront of my realities and realize that it was true that Michael had passed!!! One sweet spirit that touched the world through music. We are all blessed to have been witness to what true humanitarian can and should look like. LOVE YOU MICHAEL!!! UNTOUCHABLE YOU!!!"

Comment ~ Jean A. Scott-"I felt overwhelmed, I feel like I lost a family member."

Dear Fans, There are no words to describe the pain that this lost have brought to you and your reaction when you heard the news. Some of you may never be the same. A part of has died the day Michael passed away. It left a hole in my heart. That is why I had to publish this book. Therefore, I pray that this book have brought some joy to you also. Michael will forever live in our hearts. He will never die to his true fans. May it give you some peace. Psalms 147:3 He heals the brokenhearted, and binds up their wounds.

PHOTO ALBUM

PHOTO ALBUM

PHOTO ALBUM

PHOTO ALBUM

PHOTO ALBUM

Blender described Michael Jackson as the "late twentieth century pre-eminent pop icon"

PHOTO ALBUM

In "Billie Jean", Michael sings about an obsessive fan who alleges he has fathered a child of hers.

PHOTO ALBUM

PHOTO ALBUM

PHOTO ALBUM

PHOTO ALBUM

PHOTO ALBUM

"REMEMBER THE TIME"

PHOTO ALBUM

PHOTO ALBUM

Time noted, "Jackson is the biggest thing since The Beatles. He is the hottest single phenomenon since Elvis Presley. He just may be the most popular black singer ever".

PHOTO ALBUM

PHOTO ALBUM

PHOTO ALBUM

PHOTO ALBUM

The New York Times gave the opinion that he was a "musical phenomenon", and that "in the world of pop music, there is Michael Jackson and there is everybody else"

PHOTO ALBUM

"Bad" album:

"Bad" (1987)

Written and Composed
Michael Jackson

Your Butt Is Mine
Gonna Take You Right
Just Show Your Face
In Broad Daylight
I'm Telling You
On How I Feel
Gonna Hurt Your Mind
Don't Shoot To Kill
Come On, Come On,
Lay It On Me All Right...
I'm Giving You
On Count Of Three
To Show Your Stuff
Or Let It Be . . .
I'm Telling You
Just Watch Your Mouth
I Know Your Game
What You're About
Well They Say The Sky's
The Limit
And To Me That's Really True
But My Friend You Have
Seen Nothing
Just Wait 'Til I Get Through . . .

Because I'm Bad, I'm Bad-
Come On
(Bad Bad-Really, Really Bad)
You Know I'm Bad, I'm Bad-
You Know It
(Bad Bad-Really, Really Bad)
You Know I'm Bad, I'm Bad-
Come On, You Know
(Bad Bad-Really, Really Bad)
And The Whole World Has To
Answer Right Now
Just To Tell You Once Again,
Who's Bad . . .

The Word Is Out
You're Doin' Wrong
Gonna Lock You Up
Before Too Long,
Your Lyin' Eyes
Gonna Take You Right
So Listen Up
Don't Make A Fight,
Your Talk Is Cheap
You're Not A Man
You're Throwin' Stones
To Hide Your Hands
But They Say The Sky's
The Limit
And To Me That's Really True
And My Friends You Have
Seen Nothin'
Just Wait 'Til I Get Through . . .
Because I'm Bad, I'm Bad-
Come On

(Bad Bad-Really, Really Bad)
You Know I'm Bad, I'm Bad-
You Know It
(Bad Bad-Really, Really Bad)
You Know I'm Bad, I'm Bad-
You Know It, You Know
(Bad Bad-Really, Really Bad)
And The Whole World Has To
Answer Right Now

(And The Whole World Has To Answer Right Now)
Just To Tell You Once Again,
(Just To Tell You Once Again)
Who's Bad . . .
We Can Change The World Tomorrow
This Could Be A Better Place
If You Don't Like What I'm Sayin'
Then Won't You Slap My Face . . .

Because I'm Bad, I'm Bad- Come On
(Bad Bad-Really, Really Bad)
You Know I'm Bad, I'm Bad- You Know It
(Bad Bad-Really, Really Bad)
You Know I'm Bad, I'm Bad- You Know It, You Know
(Bad Bad-Really, Really Bad)
Woo! Woo! Woo!
(And The Whole World Has To Answer Right Now Just To Tell You Once Again . . .)
You Know I'm Bad, I'm Bad- Come On
(Bad Bad-Really, Really Bad)
You Know I'm Bad, I'm Bad- You Know It-You Know It

(Bad Bad-Really, Really Bad)
You Know, You Know, You Know, Come On
(Bad Bad-Really, Really Bad)
And The Whole World Has To Answer Right Now
(And The Whole World Has To Answer Right Now)
Just To Tell You
(Just To Tell You Once Again)
You Know I'm Smooth, I'm Bad, You Know It
(Bad Bad-Really, Really Bad)
You Know I'm Bad, I'm Bad Baby

(Bad Bad-Really, Really Bad)
You Know, You Know, You Know It, Come On
(Bad Bad-Really, Really Bad)
And The Whole World Has To Answer Right Now
(And The Whole World Has To Answer Right Now)
Woo!
(Just To Tell You Once Again)
You Know I'm Bad, I'm Bad- You Know It
(Bad Bad-Really, Really Bad)
You Know I'm Bad-You Know-Hoo!
(Bad Bad-Really, Really Bad)
You Know I'm Bad-I'm Bad- You Know It, You Know

(Bad Bad-Really, Really Bad)
And The Whole World Has To Answer Right Now
(And The Whole World Has To Answer Right Now)
Just To Tell You Once Again . . .
(Just To Tell You Once Again . . .) Who's Bad?

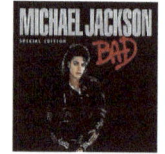

"Beat It" album:

"Thriller" (1982)

Rap by Vincent Price.
Written and composed by
Michael Jackson.

[1st Verse]
They Told Him Don't You Ever Come Around Here
Don't Wanna See Your Face, You Better Disappear
The Fire's In Their Eyes And Their Words Are Really Clear
So Beat It, Just Beat It
[2nd Verse]
You Better Run, You Better Do What You Can
Don't Wanna See No Blood, Don't Be A Macho Man
You Wanna Be Tough, Better Do What You Can
So Beat It, But You Wanna Be Bad
[Chorus]
Just Beat It, Beat It, Beat It, Beat It
No One Wants To Be Defeated
Showin' How Funky Strong Is Your Fight
It Doesn't Matter Who's Wrong Or Right
Just Beat It, Beat It
Just Beat It, Beat It
Just Beat It, Beat It
Just Beat It, Beat It
[3rd Verse]
They're Out To Get You, Better Leave While You Can
Don't Wanna Be A Boy, You Wanna Be A Man
You Wanna Stay Alive, Better Do What You Can
So Beat It, Just Beat It
[4th Verse]
You Have To Show Them That You're Really Not Scared
You're Playin' With Your Life, This Ain't No Truth Or Dare

They'll Kick You, Then They Beat You, Then They'll Tell You It's Fair
So Beat It, But You Wanna Be Bad
[Chorus]
Just Beat It, Beat It, Beat It, Beat It
No One Wants To Be Defeated
Showin' How Funky Strong Is Your Fight
It Doesn't Matter Who's Wrong Or Right
[Chorus]
Just Beat It, Beat It, Beat It, Beat It
No One Wants To Be Defeated
Showin' How Funky Strong Is Your Fight
It Doesn't Matter Who's Wrong Or Right
Just Beat It, Beat It, Beat It, Beat It, Beat It
[Chorus]
Beat It, Beat It, Beat It, Beat It
No One Wants To Be Defeated
Showin' How Funky Strong Is Your Fight
It Doesn't Matter Who's Wrong Or Right
[Chorus]
Just Beat It, Beat It, Beat It, Beat It
No One Wants To Be Defeated
Showin' How Funky Strong Is Your Fight
It Doesn't Matter Who's Wrong Or Who's Right
[Chorus]
Just Beat It, Beat It, Beat It, Beat It
No One Wants To Be Defeated
Showin' How Funky Strong Is Your Fight
It Doesn't Matter Who's Wrong Or Right
[Chorus]
Just Beat It, Beat It, Beat It, Beat It
No One Wants To Be Defeated
Showin' How Funky Strong Is Your Fight
It Doesn't Matter Who's Wrong Or Right
Just Beat It, Beat It , Beat It, Beat It, Beat It

"Ben" album: "Ben" (1972) Written by Michael Jackson

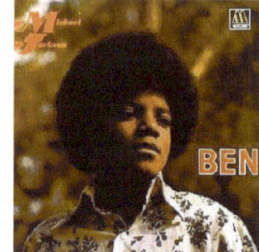

Ben, the two of us
need look no more
We both found what we were looking for
With a friend to call my own
I'll never be alone
And you my friend will see
You've got a friend in me
(You've got a friend in me)

Ben, you're always running here and there
(Here and there)
You feel you're not wanted anywhere
(Anywhere)
If you ever look behind
And don't like what you find

There's something you should know
You've got a place to go
(You've got a place to go)

I used to say "I" and "me"
Now it's "us", now it's "we"
I used to say "I" and "me"
Now it's "us", now it's "we"

Ben, most people would turn you away
I don't listen to a word they say
They don't see you as I do
I wish they would try to
I'm sure they'd think again
If they had a friend like Ben
(A friend)
Like Ben
(Like Ben)
Like Ben

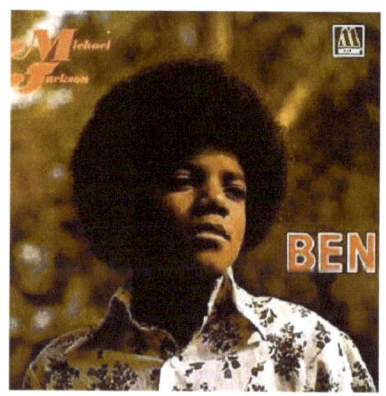

"Billie Jean" album: "Thriller" (1982)
Written by Michael Jackson

[1st Verse]
She Was More Like A Beauty Queen From A Movie Scene
I Said Don't Mind, But What Do You Mean I Am The One Who Will Dance On The Floor In The Round
She Said I Am The One Who Will Dance On The Floor In The Round

[2nd Verse]
She Told Me Her Name Was Billie Jean, As She Caused A Scene
Then Every Head Turned With Eyes That Dreamed Of Being The One
Who Will Dance On The Floor In The Round

[Bridge]
People Always Told Me Be Careful Of What You Do
And Don't Go Around Breaking Young Girls' Hearts
And Mother Always Told Me Be Careful Of Who You Love
And Be Careful Of What You Do 'Cause The Lie Becomes The Truth

[Chorus]
Billie Jean Is Not My Lover
She's Just A Girl Who Claims That I Am The One
But The Kid Is Not My Son
She Says I Am The One, But The Kid Is Not My Son

[3rd Verse]
For Forty Days And Forty Nights
The Law Was On Her Side
But Who Can Stand When She's In Demand
Her Schemes And Plans
'Cause We Danced On The Floor In The Round
So Take My Strong Advice, Just Remember To Always Think Twice
(Do Think Twice)

[4th Verse]
She Told My Baby We'd Danced 'Till Three
Then She Looked At Me
Then Showed A Photo My Baby Cried
His Eyes Looked Like Mine
Go On Dance On The Floor In The Round, Baby

[Bridge]
People Always Told Me Be Careful Of What You Do
And Don't Go Around Breaking Young Girls' Hearts
She Came And Stood Right By Me
Then The Smell Of Sweet Perfume
This Happened Much Too Soon
She Called Me To Her Room

[Chorus]
Billie Jean Is Not My Lover
She's Just A Girl Who Claims That I Am The One
But The Kid Is Not My Son
Billie Jean Is Not My Lover
She's Just A Girl Who Claims That I Am The One
But The Kid Is Not My Son
She Says I Am The One, But The Kid Is Not My Son
She Says I Am The One, But The Kid Is Not My Son
Billie Jean Is Not My Lover
She's Just A Girl Who Claims That I Am The One
But The Kid Is Not My Son
She Says I Am The One, But The Kid Is Not My Son
She Says I Am The One, She Says He Is My Son
She Says I Am The One
Billie Jean Is Not My Lover
 (6 x times)

Goon Too Soon album: **"Dangerous"** (1991)

(Written for Ryan White 1971-1990)

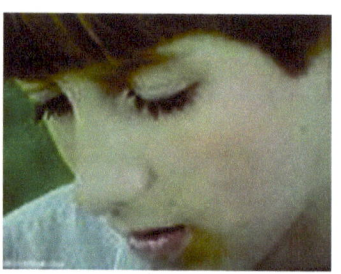

Gone Too Soon

Like A Comet
Blazing 'Cross The Evening Sky
Gone Too Soon

Like A Castle
Built Upon A Sandy Beach
Gone Too Soon

Like A Rainbow
Fading In The Twinkling Of An Eye
Gone Too Soon

Like A Perfect Flower
That Is Just Beyond Your Reach
Gone Too Soon

Shiny And Sparkly
And Splendidly Bright
Here One Day
Gone One Night

Born To Amuse, To Inspire, To Delight
Here One Day
Gone One Night
Like A Sunset

Like The Loss Of Sunlight
On A Cloudy Afternoon

Dying With The Rising Of The Moon
Gone Too Soon
Gone Too Soon

"Heal The World"
album: "Dangerous"
(1991)

There's A Place In Your Heart
And I Know That It Is

Love And This Place Could
Be Much
Brighter Than Tomorrow
And If You Really Try
You'll Find There's No Need
To Cry
In This Place You'll Feel
There's No Hurt Or Sorrow

There Are Ways
To Get There
If You Care Enough
For The Living
Make A Little Space
Make A Better Place...

Heal The World
Make It A Better Place
For You And For Me
And The Entire Human Race

There Are People Dying

If You Care Enough
For The Living
Make A Better Place
For You And For Me

If You Want To Know Why

There's A Love That
Cannot Lie
Love Is Strong
It Only Cares For
Joyful Giving
If We Try
We Shall See
In This Bliss
We Cannot Feel
Fear Or Dread
We Stop Existing And
Start Living

Then It Feels That Always
Love's Enough For
Us Growing
So Make A Better World
Make A Better World...

Heal The World
Make It A Better Place
For You And For Me
And The Entire Human Race
There Are People Dying
If You Care Enough
For The Living
Make A Better Place
For You And For Me

And The Dream We Were
Conceived In
Will Reveal A Joyful Face
And The World We
Once Believed In
Will Shine Again In Grace
Then Why Do We Keep
Strangling Life
Wound This Earth
Crucify Its Soul
Though It's Plain To See
This World Is Heavenly
Be God's Glow

We Could Fly So High
Let Our Spirits Never Die
In My Heart
Feel You Are All
My Brothers
Create A World With
No Fear
Together We'll Cry
Happy Tears
See The Nations Turn
Their Swords
Into Plowshares

We Could Really Get There
If You Cared Enough
For The Living
Make A Little Space
To Make A Better Place...

Heal The World
Make It A Better Place
For You And For Me
And The Entire Human Race
There Are People Dying
If You Care Enough
For The Living
Make A Better Place
For You And For Me

Heal The World
Make It A Better Place
For You And For Me
And The Entire Human Race
There Are People Dying
If You Care Enough
For The Living
Make A Better Place
For You And For Me

Heal The World
Make It A Better Place

For You And For Me	For You And For Me	You And For Me
And The Entire Human Race		You And For Me
There Are People Dying	There Are People Dying	You And For Me
If You Care Enough	If You Care Enough	You And For Me
For The Living	For The Living	You And For Me
Make A Better Place	Make A Better Place	You And For Me
For You And For Me	For You And For Me	You And For Me
There Are People Dying		You And For Me
If You Care Enough	You And For Me	
For The Living	You And For Me	
Make A Better Place	You And For Me	

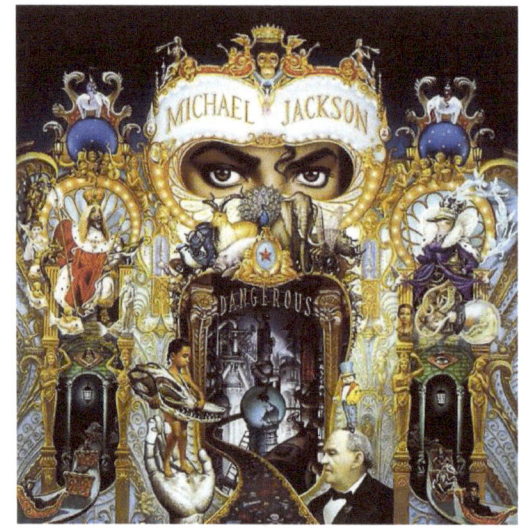

"Heaven Can Wait"
album: **"Invincible"**
(2001) Written and
Composed by

[CHORUS]

Tell the angels no, I don't wanna leave my baby alone
I don't want nobody else to hold you
That's a chance I'll take
Baby I'll stay, Heaven can wait
No, if the angels took me from this earth
I would tell them bring me back to her
It's a chance I'll take, maybe I'll stay
Heaven can wait

You're beautiful
Each moment spent with you is simply wonderful
This love I have for you girl it's incredible
And I don't know what I'd do, if I can't be with you
The world could not go on so every night I pray
If the Lord should come for me before I wake
I wouldn't wanna go if I can't see your face, can't hold you close
What good would Heaven be
If the angels came for me I'd tell them no

[CHORUS]

Unthinkable
Me sitting up in the clouds and you are all alone
The time might come around when you'd be moving on
I'd turn it all around and try to get back down to my baby girl
Can't stand to see nobody kissing, touching her
Couldn't take nobody loving you the way we were
What good would Heaven be
If the angels come for me I'd tell them no

[CHORUS]

Oh no, can't be without my baby
Won't go, without her I'd go crazy
Oh no, guess Heaven will be waiting
Ooh
Oh no, can't be without my baby
Won't go, without her I'd go crazy
Oh no, guess Heaven will be waiting
Ooh

[CHORUS]

Just leave us alone, leave us alone
Please leave us alone

"Human Nature" album: "Thriller"

(1982) Written and Composed by Steve Porcaro and John Bettis.

[1st Verse]
Looking Out
Across The Night-Time
The City Winks A Sleepless Eye
Hear Her Voice
Shake My Window
Sweet Seducing Sighs

[2nd Verse]
Get Me Out
Into The Night-Time
Four Walls Won't Hold Me Tonight
If This Town
Is Just An Apple
Then Let Me Take A Bite

[Chorus]
If They Say -
Why, Why, Tell 'Em That Is Human Nature
Why, Why, Does He Do Me That Way
If They Say -
Why, Why, Tell 'Em That Is Human Nature
Why, Why, Does He Do Me That Way

[3rd Verse]
Reaching Out
To Touch A Stranger
Electric Eyes Are Ev'rywhere
See That Girl
She Knows I'm Watching
She Likes The Way I Stare

[Chorus]
If They Say -
Why, Why, Tell 'Em That Is Human Nature
Why, Why, Does He Do Me That Way
If They Say -
Why, Why, Tell 'Em That Is Human Nature
Why, Why, Does He Do Me That Way
I Like Livin' This Way
I Like Lovin' This Way

[4th Verse]
Looking Out
Across The Morning
The City's Heart Begins To Beat
Reaching Out
I Touch Her Shoulder
I'm Dreaming Of The Street

[Chorus]
If They Say -
Why, Why, Tell 'Em That Is Human Nature
Why, Why, Does He Do Me That Way
If They Say -
Why, Why, Tell 'Em That Is Human Nature
Why, Why, Does He Do Me That Way
I Like Livin' This Way

[Repeat Chorus - Ad-Lib/Fade-Out]

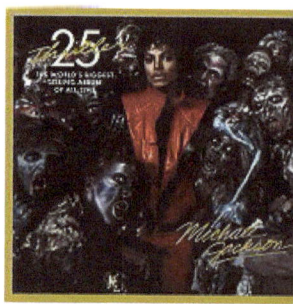

"Man In The Mirror"
album: **"Bad"** (1987)
Featuring Siedah Garret, The Winans and The Andrae Crouch Choir
Written and Composed by Siedah Garrett and Glen Ballard.

I'm Gonna Make A Change,
For Once In My Life
It's Gonna Feel Real Good,
Gonna Make A Difference
Gonna Make It Right . . .

As I, Turn Up The Collar On My
Favourite Winter Coat
This Wind Is Blowin' My Mind
I See The Kids In The Street,
With Not Enough To Eat
Who Am I, To Be Blind?
Pretending Not To See Their Needs
A Summer's Disregard,
A Broken Bottle Top
And A One Man's Soul
They Follow Each Other On Me (Starting With Me!)

I'm Starting With The Man In The Mirror
(Ooh!)
I'm Asking Him To Change His Ways
(Ooh!)
And No Message Could Have Been Any Clearer
If You Wanna Make The World A Better Place
(If You Wanna Make The World A Better Place)
The Wind Ya' Know
'Cause They Got Nowhere To Go
That's Why I Want You To Know

I'm Starting With The Man In The Mirror
I'm Asking Him To Change His Ways
And No Message Could Have Been Any Clearer
If You Wanna Make The World A Better Place
(If You Wanna Make The World A Better Place)
Take A Look At Yourself, And Then Make A Change
(Take A Look At Yourself, And Then Make A Change)
Take A Look At Yourself And Then Make A Change
(Take A Look At Yourself And Then Make A Change)

I'm Starting With The Man In The Mirror
(Ooh!)
I'm Asking Him To Change His Ways
(Change His Ways-Ooh!)
And No Message Could've Been Any Clearer
If You Wanna Make The World
(Na Na Na, Na Na Na, Na Na, Na Nah) I've Been A Victim Of A Selfish
Kind Of Love
It's Time That I Realize
That There Are Some With No Home, Not A Nickel To Loan
Could It Be Really Me,
Pretending That They're Not Alone?

A Willow Deeply Scarred,
Somebody's Broken Heart
And A Washed-Out Dream
(Washed-Out Dream)
They Follow The Pattern Of The Wind, Ya' See
Cause They Got No Place To Be
That's Why I'm Starting With A Better Place
(If You Wanna Make The World A Better Place)
Take A Look At Yourself And Then Make That . . .
(Take A Look At Yourself And Then Make That . . .)
Change!

I'm Starting With The Man In The Mirror,
(Man In The Mirror-Oh Yeah!)
I'm Asking Him To Change

His Ways
(Better Change!)
No Message Could Have
Been Any Clearer
(If You Wanna Make The
World A Better Place)
(Take A Look At Yourself And
Then Make The Change)
(You Gotta Get It Right, While
You Got The Time)
('Cause When You Close Your
Heart)
You Can't Close Your . . . Your
Mind!
(Then You Close Your . . .
Mind!)
That Man, That Man, That
Man, That Man
With That Man In The Mirror
(Man In The Mirror, Oh Yeah!)
That Man, That Man, That Man
I'm Asking Him To Change
His Ways
(Better Change!)
You Know . . . That Man
No Message Could Have
Been Any Clearer
If You Wanna Make The World
A Better Place
(If You Wanna Make The
You Know . . .
(Change . . .)
Make That Change.

World A Better Place)
Take A Look At Yourself And
Then Make A Change
(Take A Look At Yourself And
Then Make A Change)
Hoo! Hoo! Hoo! Hoo! Hoo!
Na Na Na, Na Na Na, Na Na,
Na Nah
(Oh Yeah!)
Gonna Feel Real Good Now!
Yeah Yeah! Yeah Yeah!
Yeah Yeah!
Na Na Na, Na Na Na, Na Na,
Na Nah
(Ooooh . . .)
Oh No, No No . . .
I'm Gonna Make A Change
It's Gonna Feel Real Good!
Come On!
(Change . . .)
Just Lift Yourself
You Know
You've Got To Stop It.
Yourself!
(Yeah!-Make That Change!)
I've Got To Make That Change,
Today!
Hoo!
(Man In The Mirror)
You Got To

You Got To Not Let Yourself . . .

Brother . . .
Hoo!
(Yeah!-Make That Change!)
You Know-I've Got To Get
That Man, That Man . . .
(Man In The Mirror)
You've Got To
You've Got To Move! Come
On! Come On!
You Got To . . .
Stand Up! Stand Up!
Stand Up!
(Yeah-Make That Change)
Stand Up And Lift
Yourself, Now!
(Man In The Mirror)
Hoo! Hoo! Hoo!
Aaow!
(Yeah-Make That Change)
Gonna Make That Change . . .
Come On!
(Man In The Mirror)
You Know It!
You Know It!
You Know It!

"Remember The Time"
album: **"Dangerous"**
(1991)

Do You Remember
When We Fell In Love
We Were Young
And Innocent Then
Do You Remember
How It All Began
It Just Seemed Like Heaven
So Why Did It End?

Do You Remember
Back In The Fall
We'd Be Together
All Day Long
Do You Remember
Us Holding Hands
In Each Other's Eyes
We'd Stare
(Tell Me)

Do You Remember The Time
Do You Remember The Time
When We First Met
Do You Remember The Time
When We Fell In Love
Do You Remember The Time

Remember The Times
Ooh
Remember The Times
Do You Remember Girl
Remember The Times
On The Phone You And Me
Remember The Times
Till Dawn, Two Or Three

When We Fell In Love
Do You Remember The Time
When We First Met
Do You Remember The Time
When We Fell In Love
Do You Remember The Time

Do You Remember
How We Used To Talk
(Ya Know)
We'd Stay On The Phone
At Night Till Dawn
Do You Remember
All The Things We Said Like
I Love You So
I'll Never Let You Go

Do You Remember
Back In The Spring
Every Morning Birds Would Sing
Do You Remember
Those Special Times
They'll Just Go On And On
In The Back Of My Mind
What About Us Girl

Remember The Times
Do You. Do You, Do You,
Do You, Do You
Remember The Times
In The Park, On The Beach
Remember The Times
You And Me In Spain
Remember The Times
What About, What About...

Remember The Times
Ooh... In The Park

Do You Remember The Time
When We Fell In Love
Do You Remember The Time
When We First Met Girl
Do You Remember The Time
When We Fell In Love
Do You Remember The Time
Those Sweet Memories
Will Always Be Dear To Me
And Girl No Matter What Was Said
I Will Never Forget What We Had
Now Baby

Do You Remember The Time
When We Fell In Love
Do You Remember The Time
When We First Met
Do You Remember The Time
When We Fell In Love
Do You Remember The Time

Do You Remember The Time
When We Fell In Love
Remember The Times
After Dark..., Do You, Do You,
Do You
Remember The Times
Do You, Do You, Do You, Do
You
Remember The Times
Yeah Yeah
Remember The Times

"Speechless" album: **"Invincible"** (2001)

Your love is magical, that's how I feel
But I have not the words here to explain
Gone is the grace for expressions of passion
But there are worlds and worlds of ways to explain
To tell you how I feel

But I am speechless, speechless
That's how you make me feel
Though I'm with you I am far away and nothing is for real

When I'm with you I am lost for words, I don't know what to say
My head's spinning like a carousel, so silently I pray
Helpless and hopeless, that's how I feel inside
Nothing's real, but all is possible if God is on my side

When I'm with you I am in the light where I cannot be found
It's as though I am standing in the place called Hallowed Ground Speechless, speechless, that's how you make me feel

Though I'm with you I am far away and nothing is for real I'll go anywhere and do anything just to touch your face There's no mountain high I cannot climb I'm humbled in your grace

Speechless, speechless, that's how you make me feel
Though I'm with you I am lost for words and nothing is for real

Speechless, speechless, that's how you make me feel
Though I'm with you I am far away, and nothing is for real

Speechless, speechless, that's how you make me feel
Though I'm with you I am lost for words and nothing is for real

Speechless Your love is magical, that's how I feel
But in your presence I am lost for words
Words like, "I love you."

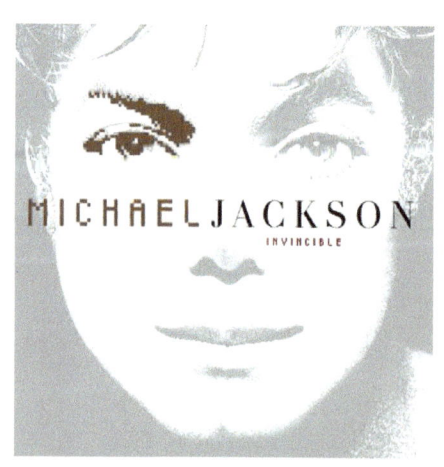

"Thriller" album:
"Thriller" (1982)

It's close to midnight and something evil's lurking in the dark

Under the moonlight, you see a sight that almost stops your heart
You try to scream but terror takes the sound before you make it
You start to freeze as horror looks you right between the eyes
You're paralyzed

'Cause this is thriller, thriller night
And no one's gonna save you from the beast about strike
You know it's thriller, thriller night
You're fighting for your life inside a killer, thriller tonight

You hear the door slam and
Thriller, thriller night
So let me hold you tight and share a Killer, diller, chiller, thriller here tonight

'Cause this is thriller, thriller night
Girl, I can thrill you more than any ghost would ever dare try
Thriller, thriller night
So let me hold you tight and share

And though you fight to stay alive
Your body starts to shiver
For no mere mortal can resist

Rap by Vincent Price. Written and composed by Rod Temperton

realize there's nowhere left to run
You feel the cold hand and

wonder if you'll ever see the sun
You close your eyes and hope that this is just imagination, girl!
But all the while you hear the creature creeping up behind
You're out of time

'Cause this is thriller, thriller night
There ain't no second chance against the thing with forty eyes, girl
Thriller, thriller night
You're fighting for your life inside a killer, thriller tonight

Night creatures calling, the dead start to walk in their masquerade
There's no escaping the jaws of a killer, thriller, ow!
(I'm gonna thrill ya tonight)
Darkness falls across the land
The midnight hour is close at hand Creatures crawl in search of blood To terrorize y'alls neighborhood

I'm gonna thrill ya tonight, ooh baby

the alien this time
(They're open wide)
This is the end of your life

They're out to get you, there's demons closing in on every side
They will possess you unless you change that number on your dial
Now is the time for you and I to cuddle close together, yeah
All through the night I'll save you from the terror on the screen
I'll make you see

That this is thriller, thriller night
'Cause I can thrill you more than any ghost would ever dare try

I'm gonna thrill ya tonight, oh darlin'
Thriller night, baby, ooh!

The foulest stench is in the air
The funk of forty thousand years
And grizzly ghouls from every tomb
Are closing in to seal your doom

The evil of the thriller (laughter)

"We're The World (USA For Africa)"

There comes a time when we hear a certain call

When the world must come together as one

There are people dying

and it's time to lend a hand to life

There greatest gift of all

We can't go on pretending day by day

That someone, somewhere will soon make a change

We are all a part of God's great big family

And the truth, you know,

Love is all we need

[Chorus:]

We are the world, we are the children

We are the ones who make a brighter day

So let's start giving

There's a choice we're making

We're saving our own lives

it's true we'll make a better day

Just you and me

Send them your heart so they'll know that someone cares

And their lives will be stronger and free

As God has shown us by turning stones to bread

So we all must lend a helping hand

[Chorus]

When you're down and out, there seems no hope at all

But if you just believe there's no way we can fall

Let us realize that a change can only come

When we stand together as one

[Chorus]

Maya Angelou's Poem Tribute to Michael Jackson:

Present by Queen Latifah at the Michael Jackson public Memorial on Tuesday, July 7, 2009

'We Had Him'

Beloveds, now we know that we know nothing,
Now that our bright and shining star can slip away from our fingertips
Like a puff of summer wind.

Without notice, our Dear Love can escape our doting embrace.
Sing our songs among the stars and walk our dances across the face of the moon.

In the instant that Michael is gone, we know nothing.
No clocks can tell time.
No oceans can rush our tides with the abrupt absence of our treasure.

Though we are many, each of us is achingly alone, piercingly alone.
Only when we confess our confusion can we remember that he was a gift to us
And WE DID HAVE HIM.

(Continued)

'We Had Him'

He came to us from the creator, trailing creativity in abundance.
Despite the anguish, his life was sheathed in mother love, family love, and survived and did more than that.

He thrived with passion and compassion, humor and style.
We had him whether we know who he was or did not know,
He was ours and we were his.

We had him, beautiful, delighting our eyes.
His hat, aslant over his brow, and took a pose on his toes for all of us.
And we laughed and stomped our feet for him.

We were enchanted with his passion because he held nothing.
He gave us all he had been given.

Today in Tokyo, beneath the Eiffel Tower, in Ghana's Black Star Square.
In Johannesburg and Pittsburgh, in Birmingham, Alabama,
And Birmingham, England

We are missing Michael.

But we do know WE HAD HIM,

And we are the world.

References and Footnotes

Can You Feel It (#2 in The Netherlands in 1981)Hit Dossier 1939-1994,1994,/Top 40 Hitdossier 1956-2001,2001,ISBN 90-257-3349-2.

1. ^ ^ ISBN 90-230-0820-0
2. "Fatboy Slim's Praise You voted best video". The Guardian. 2001-07-31.. Retrieved on 2008-07-30.

Dangerous Page "Dangerous". AllMusic. http://www.allmusic.com/cg/amg.dll?p=amg&sql=10:j9foxq95ld6e. Retrieved on 2009-04-27.

1. ^ "Grammy for Bruce Swedien & Teddy Riley". Grammy. http://www.grammy.com/GRAMMY_Awards/Winners/Results.aspx. Retrieved on 2009-02-25.
2. ^ Carter, Kelley L. (2008-08-11). "New jack swing". Chicago Tribune. http://www.chicagotribune.com/features/arts/chi-5-things-0810aug10,0,1329158.story. Retrieved on 2008-08-21.
3. "Flashbacks!". beach-bulletin.com. ^. Retrieved on 2007-06-30.

Thriller Page

1. ^ a b c d e Erlewine, Stephen (February 19, 2007). "Thriller Overview". Allmusic. ^. Retrieved on June 15, 2008.
2. ^ a b Christgau, Robert (December 28, 1982). "Christgau's Consumer Guide, Dec 28th, 1982". Robert Christgau.com. http://www.robertchristgau.com/xg/cg/cgv12-82.php. Retrieved on July 3, 2008.
3. ^ a b Maker, Melody (1982). "Thriller Review". Uncut Presents NME Originals 80's (2005): 68.
4. ^ "Review: Thriller". Q (January 2000): 138.
5. ^ a b c d e f Connelly, Christopher (January 28, 1983). "Michael Jackson: Thriller". Rolling Stone. http://www.rollingstone.com/artists/michaeljackson/albums/album/303823/review/6067536/thriller. Retrieved on June 15, 2008.
6. ^ a b c Henderson, Eric (2003). "Michael Jackson: Thriller". Slant Magazine. http://www.slantmagazine.com/music/music_review.asp?ID=358. Retrieved on June 15, 2008.
7. ^ Rosenberg, Tal (19 June 2007). "Review: Thriller". Stylus Magazine. http://www.stylusmagazine.com/articles/diamond/michael-jackson-thriller.htm. Retrieved on 13 June 2009.
8. ^ a b Rockwell, John (December 19, 1982). "Michael Jackson's Thriller': Superb Job". The New York Times. http://query.nytimes.com/gst/fullpage.html?res=9E00E4D71F39F93AA25751C1A964948260. Retrieved on July 3, 2008.
9. ^ artist development
10. ^ a b "Michael Jackson Photo Gallery 迈克•杰克逊影集". BBC China. http://www.bbc.co.uk/china/learningenglish/specials/1430_jackson_photo/page7.shtml. Retrieved on July 16, 2009.
11. ^ "Grammy Award Winners". The Recording Academy. http://www.grammy.com/GRAMMY_Awards/Winners/Results.aspx?title=&winner=Michael+Jackson&year=0&genreID=0&hp=1. Retrieved on February 14, 2008.
12. ^ a b Erlewine, Stephen. "Off the Wall Overview". Allmusic. http://www.allmusic.com/cg/amg.dll?p=amg&sql=A7cu1z85ajyv6. Retrieved on June 15, 2008.
13. ^ a b Holden, Stephen (November 1, 1979). "Off the Wall: Michael Jackson". Rolling Stone. http://www.rollingstone.com/reviews/album/259585/review/6067502/off_the_wall. Retrieved on July 23, 2008.
14. ^ "Michael Jackson: Off the Wall - Classic albums - Music - Virgin media". Virgin Media. http://www.virginmedia.com/music/classicalbums/michaeljackson-offthewall.php. Retrieved on December 12, 2008.
15. ^ Taraborrelli, p. 196 ^ Taraborrelli, p. 206
16. ^ Taraborrelli, p. 190
17. ^ a b Taraborrelli, p. 191
18. ^ a b c Taraborrelli, pp. 220–221
19. ^ a b c d e f Jackson, Michael. Thriller Special Edition Audio.
20. ^ Taraborrelli, pp. 209–210
21. ^ a b c d e f g h "Michael Jackson's Monster Smash". The Daily Telegraph. November 25, 2007. http://www.telegraph.co.uk/arts/main.jhtml?xml=/arts/2007/11/25/sv_thriller.xml. Retrieved on April 20, 2008.
22. ^ Ebony Magazine: Michael: 25 Years After Thriller, December 2007, pg. 97–98
23. ^ a b Jackson, Michael. Interview with Jesse Jackson. March 2005.
24. ^ a b George, p. 23
25. ^ a b c d e Huey, Steve. "Michael Jackson - Biography". Allmusic. http://www.allmusic.com/cg/amg.dll?p=amg&sql=11:kifuxqe5ldae~T1. Retrieved on November 11, 2006.
26. ^ a b c d e f g Taraborrelli, pp. 223–225
27. ^ Pareles, Jon (September 1987). "Critic's Notebook; How Good Is Jackson's 'Bad'?". The New York Times. http://query.nytimes.com/gst/fullpage.html?res=9B0DE1DC1F38F930A3575AC0A961948260&n=Top%2fReference%2fTimes%20Topics%2fPeople%2fJ%2fJackson%2c%20Michael. Retrieved on April 19, 2007.
28. ^ a b c d "Michael Jackson, "Billy Jean"". Blender. October 2005. http://www.blender.com/guide/articles.aspx?ID=1777. Retrieved on April 11, 2007.
29. ^ "Michael Jackson: Biography". The New Rolling Stone Album Guide. 2004. http://www.rollingstone.com/artists/michaeljackson/biography. Retrieved on February 14, 2008.
30. ^ a b c d e f g h Cocks, Jay (March 1984). "Why He's a Thriller". Time. http://www.time.com/time/magazine/article/0,9171,950053-1,00.html. Retrieved on March 17, 2007.
31. ^ George, p. 22
32. ^ "Sold On Song Top 100". British Broadcasting Corporation. http://www.bbc.co.uk/radio2/soldonsong/songlibrary/billiejean.shtml. Retrieved on April 5, 2008.
33. ^ "Sold On Song". British Broadcasting Corporation. http://www.bbc.co.uk/radio2/soldonsong/songlibrary/thriller.shtml. Retrieved on April 5, 2008.

34. ^ "Sessions". Steve Lukather. 2006. http://www.stevelukather.net/Biography.aspx. Retrieved on April 5, 2008.
35. ^ "Grammy for Michael Jackson, Quincy Jones and Bruce Swedien". Grammy. http://www.grammy.com/GRAMMY_Awards/Winners/Results.aspx. Retrieved on February 25, 2009.
36. ^ Guinness World Records (2006). Guinness World Records 2007. New York: Guinness World Records Ltd. ISBN 1-904994-12-1.
37. ^ a b Jackson, Michael. Michael Jackson: The Ultimate Collection booklet.
38. ^ Taraborrelli, p. 482 (pictures)
39. ^ "The Billboard 200 Albums - 1983". http://www.billboard.com/bbcom/charts/yearend_chart_display.jsp?f=The+Billboard+200&g=Year-end+Albums&year=1983. Retrieved on 2009-07-07.
40. internet
41. Allmusic
42. www.allmichaeljackson.com
43. www.philly.com,
44. The Philadelphia Daily News
45. www.eLyrics.net,
46. Steve Huey
47. www.imdb.com
48. www.azlyrics.com
49. www.en.wikipedia.com,
50. www.guinnessworldrecord.com
51. www.last.fm.com
52. www.metrolyrics.com
53. www.msnbc.msn.com
54. Maya Angelou's Poem "We Had Him"
55. Facebook
56. Isseecolor

Note: Some statements may have been deleted to keep this publication positive.